INVITING CHILDREN'S AUTHORS AND ILLUSTRATORS

A How-To-Do-It Manual
For School and Public Librarians

Kathy East

HOW-TO-DO-IT MANUALS
FOR LIBRARIANS
Number 49

NEAL-SCHUMAN PUBLISHERS, INC.
New York, London

Published by Neal-Schuman Publishers, Inc.
100 Varick Street
New York, NY 10013

Printed and bound in the United States of America

Library of Congress Cataloging-in-Publication Data

East, Kathy.
Inviting children's author's and illustrators: a how-to
-do-it manual for school and public librarians/by Kathy East.
p. cm.—(A How-to-do-it manual; 49)
Includes bibliographical references and index.
ISBN 1-55570-182-5
1. School libraries—Activity programs—United States.
2. Childrens's libraries—Activity programs—United States.
3. Authors. 4. Illustrators. 5. Children—United States—Books
and reading. I. Title. II. Series: How-to-do-it manuals for libraries
: no. 49.
Z675.S3E137 199   95–16176
027.8'222'0973—dc20   CIP

With thanks to all of the authors and illustrators who share their talents so openly with children of all ages. May all visits be memorable!

CONTENTS

PREFACE

When is it that youngsters begin to understand that the words and pictures in all books are put there by people—authors and illustrators? Even more intriguing to these young people is the realization that the author and the illustrator may be living, breathing people who can tell you, in person, how they view their craft.

Reading, especially the reading of fiction, can be a very personal experience. To picture the characters and the setting, to assign a voice to each of the characters, to react, to empathize—all of these activities are very private and bond the reader and the writer on a unique level. When the elements "click" the reader says, "This book is great!"

To discuss, share, defend, and recommend a book bares our feelings and values. When a child is speaking, honesty abounds. Authors' actions are praised, questioned, and debated. Conversations will lead to the open wondering of "Why did he have to die?" or "I could have never told my parents the way he/she did!"

It is the total involvement and undying conviction of readers that move adults to consider offering children the chance to meet, know, question, and talk to the very person who created the book. The reality of seeing a favorite author—in the flesh—can have a memorable effect on the student *and* the organizer. Awe and satisfaction greatly surpass the energy expended on plans and details. Indeed, a chance to be up close and personal with an author or illustrator can be a meaningful experience.

I have written this practical manual to make this happen for you and the young people your efforts embrace.

Kathy East
Assistant Director and
Head of Children's Services
Wood County District Library

1 WHY HAVE AN AUTHOR OR AN ILLUSTRATOR VISIT?

LITERACY FOR ALL must be our goal as librarians and teachers. Study after study reinforces the fact that learning to read competently and confidently equates with success throughout life. Few argue against the belief that everyone reaps the benefit of a literate society.

Introducing literacy at an early age is a wise investment in the time spent reading to a child and the money used to purchase books. Every child should have the first-hand experience of a writer's gift for the sound and rhythm of words and the equally amazing products of an illustrator's tools. Yet, at the same time, one must realize that the lessons need to be as basic to a child's world as toys and television.

Numerous libraries have programs that offer board books to families of newborns—right at the hospital! This gift is to encourage parents to view books as a primary form of developmental stimulation. Reading and talking about the pictures, to even the youngest child, is a powerful introduction to the wonder of words and the power of pictures. Adults need to keep reading and enjoying board books and picture books with preschool children. Nothing beats the confidence and pride of a four-year old asking the librarian for Eric Carle books! A request like this comes naturally when quality books are read and shared regularly with children. The delight in books and reading must be conveyed by the adult or caregiver to make this introduction truly successful.

Even in a household where the child is surrounded by books, magazines and newspapers, it takes a long time and sometimes a specific incident or activity to bring a child to the realization that it was a person who wrote the words and created the pictures or photographs that are taken for granted in the printed materials in the home.

Author/Illustrator Visit

- Supports literacy
- Draws attention to quality writing
- Introduces children to the world of art through illustration
- Introduces children to talented and devoted men and women
- Inspires writing and art activities
- Builds self-esteem
- Enriches the library and the community

CHILDREN'S WRITING ACTIVITIES

A child's first writing activity—learning to write his or her name—is a very proud accomplishment. Extending the skill to signing Valentine or birthday cards, filling in the blanks on party invitations, and writing a simple thank you note for a gift are all personal ways to use the new-found skill of writing.

Figure 1-1: The Reason For Having Literature Related Events—Kids Who Read, Succeed

One of the most satisfying activities with young children is to help them make a book:

Take even one sheet of paper, fold it and slit the pages. Add pictures of the child or sketches of favorite toys; number the pages and label with a single word—thus, naming the child's world.

What a personal association with a book. This task is so easy and convenient that it can be repeated over and over again. Suddenly, all the printed words and signs in the outside world take on new meaning because it makes sense that all of the words surrounding this child were first put there by a writer and a new concept is put into place—a reader can also be a writer.

Just as the writing, photographs, and drawings of the people who contribute to newspapers and magazines that inundate us are so readily overlooked, so are the talents of the people who create children's books that may be a part of our everyday life. Often we have not slowed down long enough to examine or scrutinize, enjoy, and value them. Stopping to closely study the words of a book and view each illustration as a work of art begins to bring an appreciation for the talent of the people who

Figure 1-2: Workshop Flyer for Parents to Promote Reading to Children

When:
Tuesday Sept. 25, 7:00-9:30 p.m.

Where:
Douglass Elementary School,
43 Douglass, Columbus, 43205
(Three blocks east of Parsons
and E. Broad Streets)

For:
Columbus' parents with
children ages preschool to 11

Presented free
of charge

by **READING IS
FUNDAMENTAL, INC.**

through a grant
from the General
Electric Foundation

A Workshop for Parents

Feature Presentation: "Growing Up Reading" Hedda Sharapan, Associate Producer of Mr. Roger's Neighborhood T.V. Program

Talk-And-Take Home Workshops: Creative ideas to encourage your children's love of reading.

Special RIF Book Distribution: Each parent will choose one free children's book to take home.

Reservations required (Adults Only, Sorry no child care available) Registration limited to the first 250 applicants.

For more information, call: **Action for Children** 224-0222

– TEAR HERE –

Reservation Form

Yes, I want to attend the RIF
"Growing Up Reading" Workshop.
(Reservations on-first-come, first served basis)

Return By:
September 14, 1984 to:

Your child's school or to
Action for Children
92 Jefferson Avenue
Columbus, Ohio 43215

Name: _____

Address: _____

                                   City   State   Zip

Telephone: _____

Ages of Children 11 and Younger _____

Pre-Register for Talk-And-Take-Home Workshops
(Indicate top 4 choices by numbering 1-4)

___ Finding Good Books: Libraries, Bookstores & Other Sources

___ Choosing Good Books: 9-11 year olds

___ T.V. & Reading

___ Choosing Good Books: Preschoolers

___ Storytelling and Reading Aloud

___ Reading For Children With Learning and Developmental Disabilities

___ Choosing Good Books: 6-8 year olds

___ Arts, Crafts and Reading

___ Using Columbus' Resources to Boost Reading

Sponsored by:

Action for Children

We help parents find reliable child care.
92 Jefferson Ave. • Columbus, Ohio 43215 • 224-0222

made the book. When youngsters are guided through this process, young writers are inspired—the wild imagination is set free. Scribblers and doodlers are offered a palette and the crafters of words feel that there is someplace for their stories to be printed.

A library which demonstrates that it values the people who write and illustrate children's books says a lot about itself and is certain to add to its appeal in the eyes of the public. First, such an activity shows that the library values itself and its mission to contribute to the well-being of its community. Not only will the community meet and come to appreciate this special guest, but the guest will see and interact with many individuals who will leave a lasting impression about the local quality of life. Secondly, arranging a visit shows a type of dedication—a willingness to work a little harder. Certain individuals have used their confidence, enthusiasm, and expertise to frame an impressive and special event.

When the time seems right, and inviting a real, live author or illustrator to visit is the inspiration of the moment, it is time to come down to earth and think through the best way to make it happen.

2 GETTING STARTED

Begin early—talk enthusiastically to your peers about your ideas and listen for their reaction and advice. Accept suggestions for names of authors and illustrators to invite. Remember all of your co-workers who showed positive reactions so they can be recruited later for the planning committee.

If you are in a public library, you must early on, win approval or at least get permission from your supervisor to seriously investigate an author visit. The go-ahead is probably necessary even if you have a line item in your budget for honoraria, contracts, etc. Involving the public relations and/or communications department of your library is critical and requires "top-down" administration approval. Knowing the plans of the library system as a whole may help you decide what is the best time to expect full support for your idea. Eventually the director will need to understand the goals of the visit and particularly the financial implications.

In a school, if the librarian is thinking of coordinating the event, the teachers of specific classes will need to be included in the very first plans. Again, if money is involved, those at the top must be made aware of all costs. In many schools, financial support may need to come from outside sources like the PTO (Parent-Teachers Organization) or a local business or sponsor.

When making your proposal, it may take good salesmanship on your part to convince all those whose support is needed. Try using name recognition as a selling point. Just as movie stars and recording artists have instant name recognition, so do children's book writers and illustrators. Recent award winners are names usually known to everyone. A visit by such a star would surely be a hit. A "big" name usually ensures a big audience. A "big" name will also probably ensure a higher price! Popular demand often sends daily honoraria costs skyrocketing. Sometimes having a steep honorarium is the easiest way for the most popular authors and artists to limit their invitations. Instead of the guest saying *"No, I can't come those dates or for that amount of money,"* the price forces *you* to say, *"At this time our budget is limited, but maybe another time."* Set your sights high, but do not be surprised if your first choice celebrities are already booked or are not doing visits this year.

Think big! Expect that you may need big bucks and ask for them. You may not get the money on the first request, but then again you may get more than you ever expected.

Getting financial support is not your only hurdle. Building support among your staff for the notion of an author/illustrator visit is

Who Needs To Buy Into This Decision?

* Test the waters by asking co-workers what they think

* Ask permission to investigate an author/illustrator visit

* Take into account funding sources

* Be realistic about limitations

What Is Gained?

- Reading is the focus
- The world of books and artists is expanded for youngsters
- A very personal relationship with the visiting author/illustrator is established
- The talents used in writing and illustrating are explained and become valued
- The visit is a very special event
- The visit can help make children aware of their creative potential
- "Owning" a piece of the guest's talent—for example, a book that person has written, illustrated, or both—becomes a highlight of the visit

critical. Their enthusiasm serves as positive publicity and thus improves the potential for a good attendance at your presentation.

No matter where you work, administration and board support spells success. The administration and board members need to know how unique the event really is. You need to make them proud to be part of such a special event. Board support also provides planners with the motivation to do a good job.

When you meet with anyone who needs to become a supporter, plan to take along for a first hand look, some of the books written or illustrated by your possible guest or guests. A publisher's flyer or a copy of a page from *Something About The Author* (Gale Research Co., Detroit) and a first hand account of a successful visit by this "star" to an event you attended will serve you well as added ammunition.

Interest in reading gets a shot in the arm when an author or illustrator makes an appearance. Once again the importance of books and the joy of reading is emphasized. This beautiful and rewarding link doesn't just happen for every child the first time he or she is part of an author or illustrator visit. In fact, it may take several opportunities to meet authors before the idea of books and reading and a real person connect. Yet when that "spark" is lit, the rewards are immeasurable!

For many youngsters, this personal visit is an introduction to a writer or illustrator whom they have never known or even heard of. However, the teacher or librarian should familiarize the children with that person's works before the visit. This introduction may begin a match of author and reader that would never have happened otherwise. What an exciting thing to witness!

Special visits made to libraries and schools are just like having company. Every nook and cranny is made ready. All are on their best behavior. Many youngsters dress up for this special visitor and best manners are stressed. The daily routine is adjusted. All indications are that "something special is happening." This attention to detail and the underlying message of the need to make a good impression makes self-esteem rise. Sharing this anticipation reinforces a sense of family or community.

It is also assumed that the guest is anticipating this visit as something special. After all, this is their first visit! The guest has every right to be nervous about what will be presented and whether it will be perfect for this audience. Guests want to be liked personally and want their books to be well-liked too. So guests dress up a bit too. They expend a lot of energy to reach everyone in the audience. All of this enables each person in the audience at least the momentary thought that this talented person cared enough to visit *me* and to meet *me* face to face.

KEEPSAKES FROM THE VISIT

A tangible object that can be taken home and admired over and over again is the best example of a keepsake of a visit. Almost nothing beats a personalized and autographed copy of a favorite book done by the guest author or illustrator. It is necessary to make available for purchase both hardback and paperback copies of the guest's books. Getting books on consignment through the publisher is a relatively easy way to provide a supply of the books. Publishers usually discount the books' original prices—which is a wonderful way to make books more affordable for children and their families. Also, because publishers offer discounts of up to 40 percent on these books, sales can be used as a way to raise funds for the author visit.

Having autographed copies available for drawings or door prizes is a way to get books into the hands of children who might not be able to afford them. Perhaps an anonymous donor would match a child's contribution toward buying a book or even make up the difference in price. Such actions can be handled discretely and the impact made on the child's self-esteem and joy in owning a book will grow in leaps and bounds.

Many authors and illustrators have unique autographs—everything from an illegible scrawl to charming little drawings or cartoons accompanying their name. To own, hold, and admire such a signature is a positive and cherished moment for a child.

Figure 2-1: Bookmark Illustrated By Pat Cummings

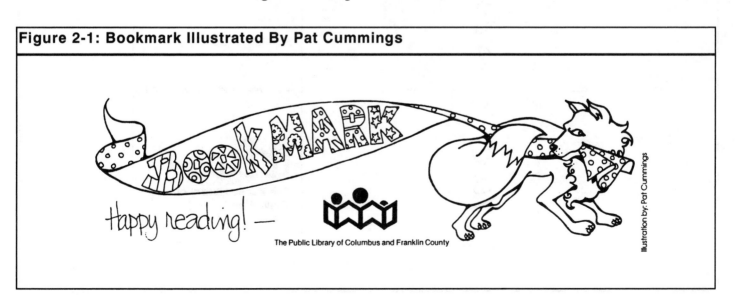

Figure 2-2: Bookmark Signed and Illustrated by Kevin Henkes with a Listing of Other Titles Written by Him on the Back

Ask your children's librarian about these books by Kevin Henkes

- All Alone

- Bailey Goes Camping

- Clean Enough

- Grandpa & Bo

- Margaret & Taylor

- Return to Sender

- A Weekend with Wendell

The Public Library of Columbus & Franklin County

Figure 2-3: Bookmark Signed By Eloise Greenfield with Her Photo and a Brief Biography on the Back

I met Eloise Greenfield
at the
Livingston Library

Thursday, Jan. 28, 1988

To my friends

*With love,
Eloise Greenfield*

1988

Eloise
Greenfield

Eloise Greenfield is the author of 17 books for children. A strong proponent of racism-free, nourishing children's literature, Ms. Greenfield has received several awards for her books, including the Coretta Scott King Award for "Africa Dream" and the Carter G. Woodson Award for her biography of "Rosa Parks." Her collection of poetry, "Honey, I Love," is an American Library Association Notable Book.

Ms. Greenfield lives in Washington, D.C., where she has taught creative writing to children under the auspices of the D.C. Commission on the Arts and Humanities. She is a member of the African American Writers Guild. Her newest works, "Under the Sunday Tree," a collection of poetry, and "Grandpa's Face," a picture book, will be published next fall.

Public Library of Columbus & Franklin County

Often in a child's eyes, he or she feels a special connection to the author or illustrator when they know a secret or some detailed or unusual fact about the guest and how the stories or pictures are created. There is a striking sense of pride and delight in being let in on an idiosyncrasy or personal tidbit—for example, knowing that Daniel Pinkwater came to visit Ohio because he had never been to a White Castle hamburger restaurant that far west made his visit very personal to his devoted fan club!

MEETING AUTHORS AND ILLUSTRATORS

Getting Information on Whom To Invite

- Attend conferences
- Request author/illustrator address and fee lists from children's books publicity departments
- Attend programs presented by authors and illustrators
- Visit publishers' exhibit booths
- Talk to publicity people in publishing companies about your school or library's special needs.
- Collect publishers' brochures
- Study publishers' catalogs

One of the reasons for being involved professionally in a library or educational organization is to reap the benefits of their regional, statewide, and national conferences or conventions. Oftentimes authors and illustrators are guests, presenters, and the recipients of special awards or other kinds of recognition at those meetings.

Events at conferences may serve as your first introduction to many authors and illustrators. Although they are usually addressing adult audiences, you can get a feel for their presence, their philosophy and attitude about what they do, insight into how they work, where they get their ideas from the messages and commitment they have to children, and especially their enthusiasm and delivery style. Take note of the luncheons and programs where authors and illustrators are speaking and plan to attend those sessions.

Many colleges and universities hold children's literature conferences, often in cooperation with their schools of education. Several authors or illustrators, book reviewers, storytellers, and other talented performers, like puppeteers and mimes, are featured speakers or give workshops. Take note of these in-service training or continuing education opportunities and try to attend. They may prove to be wonderful resources for your future planning.

Read the local newspapers and watch for author visits to bookstores, department stores, or other libraries. Try to attend some of these events to familiarize yourself with authors and illustrators you may not know. You might also gain some handy tips on how to handle a visit (or how not to.)

When you are attending these events, you can be mentally mixing and matching the presenters' skills with situations close to you—is there a certain part of your library's collection that needs new titles or recognition? Do you know of a school where a certain topic is studied in-depth? Has a PTO asked to share a visit or asked you to recommend an artist in residence for their Right-to-Read Week activities? This linkage building in your mind and the vision of a certain author or illustrator in your community are good mental calisthenics!

If authors and illustrators are not at the professional meeting you attend, there may well be publishers' representatives in the various booths at the exhibit hall. These folks are usually well acquainted with their company's stars. Even when the exhibit representative is the local sales representative, you can often get leads on which authors and illustrators are making the rounds. Also, publishing houses are almost always willing to refer you to specific schools or libraries that have hosted an author recently. In fact, you may get in touch with a particular librarian at the conference. It is possible that a face-to-face chat for fifteen minutes will tell you more than a third party letter or a phone conversation ever could.

CONTACTING THE PUBLISHER

One of the best ways to find out about authors and illustrators who are willing to visit schools and libraries is by calling the marketing people at various publishing houses. Occasionally book publishers have book promotional tours for an author coinciding with the release of a new book. The trips are usually centered around major media markets (large cities) where radio and television interviews and appearances can be arranged. If you are in such a marketing area you may be able to request a visit and avoid having to pay for the author's transportation and hotel costs.

Publishers also put out many different kinds of free promotional materials about their authors and illustrators. These brochures, bookmarks, posters, etc. have the type of background and promotional information available in *Something About the Author* or *Contemporary Authors* (Gale Research Co., Detroit). The materials are often available one year or more before biographical sketches appear in reference tools. This information is especially helpful when authors or artists are new to the field or have recently been recognized for their work—it complements the information found on book jackets. Pick up all of these handouts at conferences and meetings and keep them in a file. You may also find the publishers handouts can be the most up-to-date source for addresses when youngsters write fan letters to favorite authors and illustrators.

Publishers' catalogs are full of information about the company's writers too. Often times along with a short plot summary and an illustration from a new book, there is background information about the author and illustrator—for example, educational background, where they reside, other titles or at least the other books they have published with this particular publishing house. Some catalogs even have a page with the names of authors and illustrators currently living in the various states or regions of the United States and the world.

PRELIMINARY PLANNING FOR YOUR AUTHOR/ILLUSTRATOR VISIT

Planning/Advisory Committee Members

- You
- Another staff member or a representative from the other agency if you are doing this as part of a cooperative effort
- School or public librarian (depending on which one you are, so both are represented)
- Teacher, university contact
- Representative from a funding group
- Public relations or publicity coordinator
- Any other hard workers you believe you need or can recruit

Early in the planning stages, form a planning or advisory committee of a half-dozen or so people. This group will need to meet regularly to monitor plans and to assist with decisions. This committee can also assume specific tasks delegated by the chair. In turn, they may call upon others to assist them with their particular responsibility. The planning committee will be of great assistance. It will be comforting to have others informed of what is being planned. They can also serve as watchdogs, remind you of perhaps forgotten details, and offer encouragement. A smoothly functioning committee will also bond among themselves and find the work and camaraderie to be a rewarding experience. For some people it can serve as a training ground for being in charge of future author/illustrator visits. If you see only yourself performing all of the tasks listed for this committee, a visit can still become a reality, but try to recruit some support and assistance, if only for moral support. The more people who feel some responsibility for the success of the visit, the better.

LIBRARY AND SCHOOL PLANNING COMMITTEES

In a large public library system the planning committee might be the children's services coordinator, the children's librarians from several locations, the public relations person, and a representative on behalf of the Friends of the Library or any other funding resource.

When a group of schools share an author visit, the school librarians from each building can serve as the planning committee along with a couple of teachers and representatives from the PTOs involved.

BRAINSTORMING NAMES

Get your planning committee together and ask: *If you could invite any of the wonderful authors or illustrators of children's books, who would you ask?* If you put six people together in a room you will have a wish list in no time!

The following criteria may influence your choices:

- Name recognition—is this someone whose name every child and teacher will recognize?

- Appeal to all ages—does this person write and/or illustrate books that appeal to all ages?

- Award winners—have the names of these people been in the news because they have been honored with awards from professional organizations?

- Well-known in your state (their home state)—local celebrities are often overlooked in their home area.

- Their works match a theme or program plan you have for this event—special celebrations or events may be enhanced by a special guest.

- Person will be in your area for another commitment—sometimes relatives in your area can assist you in getting an author to visit.

- You have recently taken notice of this person and would like to get to know this creator and his/her work better.

- You have heard this person at a recent library or professional function.

- You are trying to attract a certain audience to the library (parents, teens etc.) and want just the right person.

- You want to establish a cooperative venture with an agency/organization and your suggestion would be acceptable or attractive to all involved.

- You want to feature a certain type of literature and this person exemplifies quality in this area.

- Someone has called you and suggested you share this guest's visit to the area.

- You don't have any ideas for specific names—you just want to try to host an author or illustrator.

You may be lucky enough to be located in a part of the country which has a famous landmark, a renowned science center, a unique museum or a collection of materials or some singular attraction that would be appealing to the author or illustrator you would like to invite. Make sure you include this information in your invitation. It could be the deciding factor to tip the decision in your favor.

SETTING YOUR PLAN IN MOTION

Before the brainstorming meeting is over, you need to prioritize the list of possible guests and decide on the plans for making contacts. It should also be agreed that there is flexibility in the requests. Perhaps when talking to marketing people at the various publishing houses, you will find that honoraria requests are too high for your budget. Another librarian may tell you of an author/illustrator who will be in your area and you could piggy-back your visit. Jump at opportunities to make planning easier and a visit a reality.

You may need to be flexible about the desired dates of the visit. Before you leave your meeting develop a calendar of dates which would *not* work—for example, library conferences, dates when staff might be out of town, dates of other community events that would overshadow your event, and so on. Try not to be too rigid in the beginning. Oftentimes things work out. If you cannot be flexible about dates, make sure you make your request very early—a year or two ahead of the desired date.

Before you call a publisher you may want to check with others in your community who would also like to have an author or an illustrator visit. Consider a local bookstore, a local college or university children's literature class, a group of retired teachers, a book discussion group, or an organization of teachers of whole language. They may all be very enthusiastic. Look at these groups as possible audiences. They may help publicize your event, do some of the leg work involved in the planning, and perhaps the groups might contribute to the expenses of the visit.

Do Your Homework!

Check your library's catalog for books written or illustrated by the various people on your wish list. How many copies does your library own? What are the dates of publication? Who's the publisher? Check *Books in Print* for titles currently available. How many are available in hardback? Paperback? Both? Who are the publishers?

If your collecthion does not have books written or illustrated by your proposed guest, are you willing and able to purchase the needed books? Do you know why these works are not part of the collection? Are they older titles that may have been discarded? Did they not meet the system's selection policy? Does owning many of the books make a difference to the possible success of this event?

Before making any firm commitments, call some of your friends and ask what they know about any of the people on your list. When you are starting out, a good guideline is to invite only guests who are recommended by those whose judgment you know and trust. Be sure you or someone you know well and whose professional judgment you trust has heard your intended guest speak to an audience.

Your state library and regional library youth services consultants may be helpful. Ask the children's librarians you know who frequently attend national, state, and regional conferences and workshops for their recommendations. Your state library association's youth services divisions may also serve as resources. You may also want to review the list of proposed guests and find out where they live. The book jackets of recent titles also serve as a good source for author information.

3 INITIAL CONTACTS

MAKING THE FIRST CALLS

You can make many initial contacts by looking up a publishing house in *Books In Print* or *Literary Market Place* (R.R. Bowker/Reed Reference, New Providence, NJ), or *Children's Media Market Place* (Neal-Schuman, NY) and calling their 800 number. Be patient! The first call may prove frustrating. Often you are put on hold or transferred from one office to another. Switchboard operators are busy and want to connect you quickly to someone before they answer the next call. With voice mail you may feel even more frustrated because you can leave a message, but you aren't sure that you have reached the right person, if your call will be returned, or how soon you might hear back. Plus, everyone is anxious to get an answer immediately!

You might be more successful if you ask to speak with the school library marketing person. Check any printed material you have from the specific publishing houses for the name of the person in that position. Or use the names listed in the exhibitors section in the American Library Association conference program or other such programs or listings as possible resources.

When you finally reach someone who can assist you, tell the representative something about you and your situation or needs—for example, *"I'm a children's librarian in a small public library in Nebraska. We'd like to have a children's book illustrator visit our library on the Saturday of Children's Book Week. We have $1,200 in our budget to cover all expenses."* This statement gives the representative basic information. The marketing person will have many questions to ask you. Through experience and many contacts you will find out the following information:

- Some authors and illustrators set limits on how many days or weeks they will be away from home. Some travel for four weeks, and then stay home for four to six months.

- The desire and willingness to travel may be relative to deadlines already set by the publisher. A "no" may result when the author/illustrator has a new book due in the next few months. It is better to know about this deadline when you first contact the publisher, than to find out a few weeks before a scheduled visit.

- A promotional tour planned by the publisher for a new title can be very encouraging because you may be able to plan to have your visit coincide with the publication of that new title and the tour.

- Certain events are booked years in advance. Easily identifiable weeks such as National Children's Book Week, Right-to-Read Week, National Library Week and other events like these may have been reserved long before your call.

- Having the author or illustrator stop by your library on the way to or from another event (piggy-backing) may be a good way to ensure a visit.

Plan to be flexible if you can. That will increase your chances for a positive contact.

The marketing people may discuss your request with the author's editor, who will know whether there are scheduling commitments and conflicts already on the calendar. Everything will probably not be settled with one phone call. In fact, plan for several calls. Make sure you obtain the marketing representative's name and address so that you can send a thank you and copy all future correspondence to the publisher.

CONTACTING AUTHORS OR ILLUSTRATORS DIRECTLY

Unless you are personal friends, it is better not to call authors or illustrators directly, but rather to make contact through a publisher or a third party. After all, you would not want to interrupt a moment of inspiration! In these days of answering machines and voice mail, direct contact may be unrealistic anyway.

In your community you may know or have a friend who knows the owner of a local children's bookstore who has had a local author or illustrator visit for an autographing session. These people may act as intermediaries and either make the initial contact, supply you with a phone number and an address, or give you clues or advice on what to expect if you have their friend visit your library. You can also check with other librarians in your area or state who have had author visits and ask for recommendations and information on how to get in contact with potential guests.

Worksheet 3-1: Questions to Ask When Planning A Visit

Questions You Should Ask

1. What age groups does the author prefer to address?

2. Is this presentation a straight lecture with a question and answer time or does the illustrator use slides, or do a chalk-talk, or involve the children in some way?

3. How big an audience will the guest address at one time? Is one classroom at a time too many small groups? Is an auditorium assembly of 400 children okay?

4. What message does the guest want to get across to first graders? Is it a different one for sixth graders? Will a family audience of adults through preschoolers be captivated?

5. What feedback have you gotten from schools, libraries, and classrooms where the guest has visited?

6. Does the author or illustrator expect the audience to be familiar with all of his or her works and characters or will this be treated as an opportunity to introduce him or herself to this new audience?

7. How is honorarium determined? Is it by the day? Many writers and artists request $1,000 a day. Does that mean 9 A.M. to 5 P.M. or four presentations? Must all presentations be the same? Is there any way to negotiate this fee?

8. Will the author or illustrator present at more than one school or library in a day? How about evenings?

9. What about travel arrangements and expenses? Will the guest fly? Must we offer only first class? Who makes the arrangements? Can I offer a flat fee for travel and ask the individual to plan accordingly? Is a rental car needed?

10. What about the possibility of staying over a weekend to help cut airline costs? (Many publishing companies have a policy of automatically refusing this. Will the author/illustrator be an overnight guest in someone's home? Is a stay at a bed and breakfast or a university guest house okay?

11. Will you give me a phone number and/or an address so I may contact the author directly? Or will you make the initial contact and give my name and number?

12. How shall I confirm our conversation?

AUTHORS WHO SELF-PROMOTE

Occasionally, authors or illustrators will call or drop by because they are doing their own promotional work. Sometimes authors feel that the marketing staff of their publishing house are not working

---

Figure 3-1: Sample Letter to a Publisher's Representative

Wood County District Public Library • 251 N. Main St. • Bowling Green, OH 43402-2477
Telephone: 419/352-5104 • FAX: 419/354-0405

August 12, 1992

Maureen Hayes
Macmillan Publishing
856 Third Avenue
New York, NY 10022

Dear Maureen:

Thank you so much for your assistance in getting author/illustrator Pat Cummings to agree to come to Ohio this fall. CSCL (Cooperative Services for Children's Literature) thanks you.

Pat is scheduled to arrive Thursday morning, October 1st, visit a public school in Bowling Green, give an evening presentation to the CSCL 7th Annual Book & Reader Conference and on Friday make presentations at an Oregon City School and then visit with art students in a Findlay High School before flying back to New York in the early evening. She'll be busy but she says she likes it that way!

Be assured all of the groups will prepare for her visit and welcome her royally. I know from previous work with Pat that she loves her work and lovingly shares her experiences.

I've already made flight arrangements and will mail the tickets directly to Pat. We understand her honorarium is $1000 per day and our budget is built around that figure. All expenses will be handled through CSCL and the Jerome Library at Bowling Green State University. (Your friend—and mine—Bonnie Chambers is the chairperson of the CSCL Board this year.) Sales of Pat's books will be handled through Once Upon a Mind, a children's bookstore in nearby Maumee.

Walbridge Branch Library	Bradner Branch Library
108 North Main	130 North Main
Walbridge, OH 43465	Bradner, OH 43406
419/666-9900	419/288-2422

hard enough at getting them bookings so they do them on their own. However, you should know that many publishing companies freely admit that they are understaffed, and find it very difficult to promote an author who is not yet established. An increasing trend in juvenile publishing is to provide newer authors with kits to help them do some of their own promotion and publicity, particularly on a local level. When you are approached by such an author or illustrator, remain in control. Ask some of the specific questions you would have asked a publisher's representative, like, "What is your honorarium?" and "Who can I call for a recommendation on the quality of your presentation?" Thank them for contacting you, ask for a business card and say you will get back to them.

Vanity Presses and Self-Publishers

The other self-promoters could be from vanity presses—publishers who charge the authors a fee to print their book. Or it could be a person who has self-published a book in their basement. These authors often espouse a particular cause, believe they have written the definitive book, and they want to make money. It probably sounds harsh, but beware—many times these vanity press authors are people from your community. Perhaps they know someone on your board and they were told to stop by the library. You may even know them personally. Listen to their sales pitch, but maintain your standards.

The easiest solution is to ask for a copy of their book to review. Remind this person that books purchased for the library or added to the collection must meet certain book selection criteria. Sometimes small press books are printed on poor quality paper, the typesetting may be blurred, or the binding may be inappropriate for a library's mass circulation. You really need to think of all of these factors before the content of the book is considered.

If the review of the book proves negative, send a brief note and explain at least one of the major flaws. Thank the author for considering the local library, wish them well, and enclose the note and book in an envelope and send it on its way.

Local Authors

Perhaps your library has a policy or procedure for accepting the works of local authors. Work within those guidelines, but do not be forced to plan or promote less than superior quality to children through an author visit, no matter where the author lives.

Cottage Industry Folks

On the positive side, some cottage industry folks who are testing a puppet character or a set of flannel board characters and stories and are looking for honest feedback in using and improving their products' appeal with children are quite sincere. The difference between these people is that they have a softer sell and are willing to meet your schedule. Often they will donate their time or lend you their materials for your review and trial use. Those writers and crafts people willing to make an appointment and truly listen to your analysis may benefit from your time and effort. Make sure you know what you are getting yourself into—and that you are willing to give in that way.

There are positive exceptions to all warnings and guidelines. Just be aware, listen carefully, do not make any hasty promises, and follow your instincts.

4 PROGRAM PLAN

When you are recruiting for an author visit to a large library system you may want to use the guest for one or more events in various locations within the system. Create an event; hold a reception. Use the visitor's expertise as part of an in-service program for staff. Have the author visit and make presentations at several branches. Plan the author visit to coincide with the dedication of a new building, or a newly decorated children's area. Include a visit to the local children's bookstore. Offer to have your guest give a lecture to a college class.

Invite kids to bring a brown bag lunch to enjoy "Lunch on the Lawn" with an author. This event can also serve as a way to get a program scheduled during that often lost time of 11 A.M. to 1 P.M. Be creative. Authors and artists are usually receptive to any plans that promote their works. Audiences enjoy the excitement of unpredictable events. Originality makes each visit a challenge to plan and a delight for the audience.

TYPES OF EVENTS

- Author reading from newest book, followed by questions.
- Artist doing a chalk talk (drawing and telling the story).
- Storytelling for all ages assembled (often with audience participation).
- Autograph party.
- Reception—with food and drink—and informal discussion.
- Slide show and lecture.
- After lunch or after dinner speech.
- In-service training for staff/teachers.
- Speaker at dedication of a new library, branch library, school, or special book- related facility.
- Workshop on a particular topic or skill.
- Artist-in-residence at a school (varying from several days to several weeks).

The key is to use the time, talents, and notoriety of this special guest to attract as large an audience as possible. In the public library setting this can be challenging because you do not have the captive audience of the classroom in a school. Libraries can build

Figure 4-1: Sample Flyer Advertising An Author Visit

a party with
children's author/illustrator
BRINTON TURKLE

Author of "Rachel & Obadiah," "The Boy
Who Didn't Believe In Spring" and
"Deep In the Forest"

Saturday, May 4
10:00 a.m.
Reynoldsburg Library
1402 Brice Rd.
866-0075

Copies of Mr. Turkle's books will be
available for sale and autographing.

Please park at the K-Mart
adjacent to the library

Figure 4-2: Lunch on the Lawn Flyer

Munch with
children's author/illustrator
BRINTON TURKLE

Author of "Rachel & Obadiah,"
"The Boy Who Didn't Believe In Spring"
and "Deep In the Forest."

Saturday, May 4

12:30 p.m.
Hilltop Library
2955 W. Broad St.
222-7110

Bring your own sack lunch.
A free drink and treat will be provided
by the Friends of the Library. Copies of
Mr. Turkle's books will be
available for sale and autographing.

Figure 4-3: ''Chocolate Kiss'' Handout Advertising the Visit of Arnold Adoff

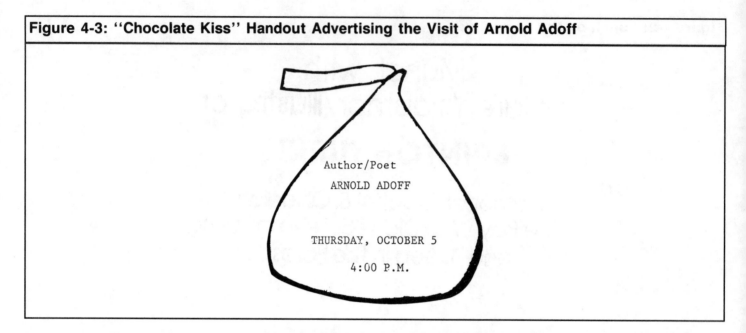

Author/Poet
ARNOLD ADOFF

THURSDAY, OCTOBER 5

4:00 P.M.

on already established, successful time slots—for example, the story time on Saturday morning which attracts preschoolers and their parents and siblings. Cooperating with child-centered agencies and holding your event in a kid-infested location will also help you assure an audience. Having a good turnout will give you satisfaction about your dollar investment in this author/illustrator's visit. If this is the first time an author or illustrator is visiting your community, the general public may not be aware of the treat in store for them. By building on a time slot when many families are already in your library, you can introduce this new event in a routine setting.

VISITS WHICH HAVE BEEN A BIG HIT

- Arnold Adoff reading from *Chocolate Dreams* (Lothrop, Lee & Shepard, 1989) and serving the audience chocolates donated by the local candy shop.

- George Ella Lyon sitting in a rocking chair and eating lunch from a basket, surrounded by an audience of children with their own baskets of lunch before she introduced the book *Basket* (Orchard, 1990).

- Seymour Simon talking informally with a class of library school students about the challenges of writing nonfiction books for young children.

- Jackie Torrence telling stories to an assembled group of 200 or so fourth, fifth, and sixth graders sitting on the floor of the school's multi-purpose room, so intrigued and quiet that the "Boo" at the end of the story really made them jump!

- Susan Terkel addressing would-be authors on how to submit manuscripts to publishers so they are noticed. She also addressed how to accept letters of rejection.

- Thomas McGregor, in full pirate regalia—surrounded by pirate flags, swords, and musical instruments—singing his way through the history and lore of piracy for four classes of fifth graders.

- Pat Cummings drawing her favorite ballerina doll—just like she did as a child—to encourage every student in the school to draw, and draw, and draw, and maybe something will come of it!

- Jean Fritz at a library dedication, delivering a poignant address demanding that all present recognize and promote the importance of becoming peacemakers.

- Wil Clay exhibiting the original paintings used in *Tailypo* (Wahl, Jan. Holt, 1991).

- Dr. T. Berry Brazelton being interviewed about health and literacy issues before a group of librarians, teachers, nurses, and health professionals. The best response was for his word by word recitation of *Goodnight Moon* (Brown, Margaret Wise. HarperCollins, 1947) when asked, What's your favorite children's book?

- Denise Fleming at the county's Young Writers Conference demonstrating papermaking, complete with pulp and screens, to show youngsters how the illustrations for *Count!* (Holt, 1992) were done.

- Sitting in the school's multi-purpose room, a tent-like structure, complete with tables and chairs, creates an intimate space for each class to sit near Jane Yolen and be entranced by her magical sharing.

- An exhibit of Wendy Parker's childhood drawings and the galleys for her book *A Christmas Doll* (Holt, Rinehart and Winston, 1979) is enhanced by a Saturday morning program with a chance to meet the author and to make a jointed paper doll or elf.

- Stopping at Cover-To-Cover bookstore with their wall of autographs and illustrations done by visiting celebrities for a small autographing party.

- A workshop on paper engineering and how pop-up books are designed and created.

Some authors and illustrators have standard presentations with which they are comfortable. You may need to adapt your plans to comply with their plans. Requesting a variety of types of presentation is perfectly okay, as long as the request is understood and accepted well beforehand by the guest.

Clearly stated expectations from all parties involved can lead to a successful and satisfying visit. Don't be afraid to ask because some of your best ideas may come directly from the artists. They have been around and have been involved in a wide range of activities. They may be very comfortable doing the offbeat or unexpected presentation. Don't hesitate to "steal" ideas or replicate the successful events of others—it's a true form of flattery!

When school librarians are planning visits or coordinating a week-long residency within a school district's five elementary schools, some attention needs to be paid to involving the whole system in the visit. Most important is letting the classroom teachers know far enough in advance who the visiting author or illustrator will be and helping the teachers get to know the books. You want the visit to be integrated into the curriculum and not to be seen as more work or as another time-consuming activity.

Having a supply of the author or illustrator's books available for the staff many months in advance of the visit enables teachers to set their own pace in getting their students familiar with the guest. This introduction launches the plans for individual classrooms. Multiple copies of all of the books can be borrowed from the public library, the college curriculum library, and other school libraries. Adequate copies for all classrooms makes reading and studying the works an easy task.

A school librarian can become an expert on the guest through research and close attention to materials supplied by the publisher. This extra effort on the part of the librarian can be quite useful in answering questions at staff meetings. The heightened awareness of a guest speaker will help smooth out bumps that may arise during a sales pitch session. A somewhat standardized format for school visits is to have two large group assemblies of one hour or so in a day. One is held in the morning and one in the afternoon to accommodate half-day kindergarten classes.

Figure 4-4: School Notification Letter of an Author Visit

Wood County District Public Library ● 251 N. Main St. ● Bowling Green, OH 43402-2477
Telephone: 419/352-5104 ● FAX: 419/354-0405

Dear Kenwood School Principal and 5th grade teachers:

The Wood County District Public Library would like to invite your fifth grade classes to a special program at the library on Friday, October 9th.

At 1:30 p.m. Thomas MacGregor, the Scottish Pirate will present the story, music and humor of the high seas and the life of a pirate. This fictitious historical account is both educational and entertaining.

Won't you be our guest? Please RSVP to the children's room, 352-5104, at the library.

Sincerely,

Kathy East

Kathy East
Head of Children's Services

Walbridge Branch Library
108 North Main
Walbridge, OH 43465
419/666-9900

Bradner Branch Library
130 North Main
Bradner, OH 43406
419/288-2442

Because the PTO usually provides funding, schools should try to find authors or illustrators who will be appealing to all of the student—from kindergartners through sixth graders. Each day some time should be allotted for a walk around the school to allow the special guest a chance to see the variety of projects and products created by the students in anticipation of his/her visit.

The remainder of the time is devoted to autographing. Sometimes the plan is to have each classroom send five or ten students at a time to the library to get their books signed. This allows for that precious moment of personal attention with the guest.

In a school only those who buy a book participate in the autographing ritual. The youngsters are limited to one book for autographing. Knowing ahead of time the number of books sold helps in estimating the amount of time needed to get all the books signed.

A nice ritual in some schools is to have the PTO provide a luncheon for the guest and the teachers. This may be in the school building or in a nearby home that offers a private, adult setting during the day.

Evenings may be organized to have small groups escort the guest to dinner, a movie, or to a special community event. Sometimes the author or illustrator prefers some "down time," alone in a hotel room. The schedule needs to be very flexible because so many factors will enter into the decisions!

BUILDING COALITIONS

HELP! is the name of the game. The idea for this event may have been yours, but its success will depend on your ability to surround yourself with people who have the same enthusiasm, commitment, knowledge, and even some financial investment in it. A broad-based committee also shares the workload and makes the final event fall into place with ease. Whatever your first reason, desire, or wish to have an author or illustrator visit may have been, it is now coming to fruition.

The excitement of an author's visit may serve as an opportunity for you to contact a group or several organizations in your community with whom you have wanted to work cooperatively and invite them to join with you. For example, an author who builds stories around children's early development may be of interest to nursing students at the closest teaching hospital as well as to the local day care center staff or the county's licensed day care home providers. Letting these people know about your plans through a personal contact can establish new coalitions.

A children's illustrator who has received national recognition may be a perfect speaker for the junior and senior high school art classes. The local community arts committee or museum may also be interested in having a program with the illustrator for their meeting. Making the contact may lead to future cooperative programs.

A service organization within the community that supports international exchange students can be invited to contribute to the financial support of the photographer who did the children's book on travel in India. Include the local photo shops when a photographer visits. The staff may want to address children about tricks in taking and improving pictures. All of these contacts open the doors for support through publicity, attendance, and dollars.

POSSIBLE GROUPS TO WORK WITH: FOR PLANNING, FUND RAISING, PUBLICITY, AND ATTRACTING AN AUDIENCE

- Branch/bookmobile staffs
- Public Library
- Local schools
- Nearby colleges and universities
- PTAs, PTOs
- Friends of the Library groups
- Local bookstore(s)
- Retired teachers
- Storytelling groups
- Pre-schools, other child service agencies
- Community service organizations
- Local businesses
- Local museums

5 Moving Ahead

Start by keeping key administrators informed of your progress. When confirmation of an author's or illustrator's visit is received, everyone's calendars should be in sync to avoid conflicts and confusion later on.

Contacts need to be made for all of the sites to be visited. The staff at all of the sites needs to be informed and be involved. Confirm program plans and draft a list of possible needs (from chairs for the audience to where does the author go after the last presentation). Commence with publicity plans and collect PR materials. Decide on printed materials needed—posters, flyers, bookmarks, and so on. Set deadline dates. Anticipate expenses—for example, will we have handouts for kids? Can one of the librarians host a cookout for supper one evening?

BUDGETING

It is time to plan and juggle the budget. When you receive a commitment of dollars from the library's Friends group, a cash donation from a library patron, a town business, or a contribution from a school PTO, each gift will need to be acknowledged. Keep your contributors informed as to how their money is being used. Do not forget to brag about cost-cutting efforts. Brag that a local motel is donating a room or that you are using a bed and breakfast to give the author a more intimate sense of the community and that the price is very reasonable.

FINDING DOLLARS

- Annually budget dollars for a visit.
- Request financial support from the Friends of the Library and the PTO's of the schools.
- Write a grant. Perhaps the local Arts Council or the Humanities Council will support particular authors/artists.
- Seek funds from local service organizations (be familiar with their pattern of philanthropic giving).
- Ask businesses and business leaders.

■ Get the word out into the community that $400 (or whatever the amount) is needed. You may be pleasantly surprised by the positive response. To plan a successful visit you must include a number of possible expenses in your budget. Become familiar with all of these and add others unique to your situation.

POSSIBLE EXPENSES

Honorarium

This is the cost for hosting an author or an illustrator visit. This fee is often negotiable. You are quoted a daily fee and that needs definition. Four presentations? Moving from classroom to classroom? Limited only to assembly gatherings? Might an evening and a half-day visit be less?

Don't hesitate to ask for specifics. An artist in residence for a week's stay should have a lower average daily fee and allow for a more flexible daily schedule. A week long stay with the same audience usually implies some kind of a finale—a special event, an end product, or an initiated project. The number of youngsters involved and the specific plans can influence the amount of the honorarium.

Travel Expenses

This includes air fare, mileage, taxi, or limousine service, and any other related fees. Check with your local travel agents on how to make air travel most economical. Distance is not always the deciding factor in the price of a flight. Price wars among the major carriers often encourage coast to coast travel. Local limitations may add to your travel costs. How near or far are you from a major airport? What expenses will you incur getting your guest from the airport to the hotel and to your library or school? Even if someone from your staff drives to the airport and back, include that mileage expense in your budget planning.

When an author or illustrator tells you what airport he or she will be using, do not forget to ask how near or far away the local airport is. Will that person drive to the airport and leave the car parked there? That mileage and parking fee is another cost to be included in your budget.

Taking a limousine or an airport shuttle is another possible expense. Although you may want to pinch every penny to keep costs to a minimum, your guest may very well plan on only the best

Budget Items

- Honorarium
- Travel expenses
- Room expenses
- Meal costs
- Local transportation
- Materials
- Equipment
- Special remembrances
- Cushion/contingency
- Books for autographing (optional) as prizes

for themselves! Somehow you need to find out about the lifestyle to which they have become accustomed.

Many potential guests are very aware of tight school and library budgets and will be frugal. However, be aware that starting with a well-rested guest will contribute to a successful visit. Therefore eliminating all of the comforts and niceties for the sake of a conservative budget should be well thought out.

Accommodations

Most visits require some kind of overnight accommodations. When possible, it is better to have the author or illustrator arrive the night before the scheduled event. That way you know the day will be off to a good start. However, busy schedules and other commitments often do not allow the luxury of an early arrival. It is necessary to build in an ample cushion of time before the first performance as planes are delayed, connections are canceled, cars break down, and other calamities pop up.

Scout out the costs of area hotels and motels. Check for local bed and breakfasts or inns. Inquire about any special rates. Are certain nights cheaper? Are discounts given for governmental agencies or units? Is it possible to receive a discount because the owners or managers have children in the school? Or as a regular user of the public library would the motel owner host an author without charge? Would a member of the Friends of the Library like to pick up this expense? Perhaps a business owner would like to donate a room as a contribution to the community. Is it possible a family would like to host the author/illustrator in their home? Sometimes you are lucky and the author has family or acquaintances in the area and they will host your guest. Make sure you ask about this alternative in advance because many people now find travel and a full schedule the next day tiring enough without having to "visit" anyone.

Strive for ways to keep this expense reasonable. Your guest may have personal requests or requirements. Health, religious, or personal preferences should be honored when possible. Offering to book a guest in a bed and breakfast in a unique neighborhood in your city may illicit a reaction which sets the tone for the style of entertaining you should plan. It is necessary to allow your guest some personal time—that means away from you and the itinerary. But do not isolate your guest. Make sure there are restaurants, shopping areas, or points of interest within walking distance of where he or she is staying.

Food/Meals

Conduct a survey to get median prices for meals in your locale to help you with your guesstimate of expenses for meals. Note that some hotels, motels, bed and breakfasts, and inns include breakfast with an overnight stay. Check with your guest—will a continental breakfast be enough to start the day? Some guests may not want to eat anything before their presentation or performance.

Someone might like to host a dinner party in their home for the author and other special guests, like the library director or the school superintendent or a personal friend in the area. Lunch might be in the school cafeteria, although that option is probably not number one in the minds of all the people involved! Having a staff potluck at lunch or dinner would enable your guest some time for adult conversation. Learn about your guests' energy level by speaking to someone who has hosted your guest previously. This kind of information could make a big difference in the schedule you plan.

The expense and consumption of alcohol may be a decision your group wants to deal with early on in the planning process. Sometimes this situation can be avoided because you are holding your events in a school building or in a public building where special licensing would be required to serve alcohol.

If your group takes a definite stand, make sure you include a statement saying this in your confirmation letter. Use a statement like, *"Our school/library policy does not allow our funds to be spent on alcoholic beverages. Therefore no spirits will be included in the social events during your visit."* Such a statement places the issue in the open, stated without reservation. Remember, what you or your part of the country assumes is common practice may not be true in other parts of the nation. In contrast, you may warn or anticipate for your guest your plans. Your letter might say, "*On Thursday evening we would like to plan a wine and cheese reception at the Fine Arts Exhibit Hall of the local college.*" Your guest may want you to know ahead of time that he or she does not want liquor served.

Local Transportation Arrangements and Costs

Public transportation may be quick and convenient in your area. It may be the only sensible choice in some urban areas. Do not be afraid to let your guest know this but be reminded that such an expectation may limit the range of sample works or the number or size of items to be carried to this visit. The use of library/school owned vehicles may mean meshing schedules and having permission granted. Budget mileage costs for the personal use of vehicles for whomever is meeting your guest or driving to the airport. Investigate the convenience and cost of using an airport limousine or public transportation from the airport to a hotel. Budget mileage expenses for transporting your guest from place to place.

Materials

Included in these costs are the production of materials such as copies of handouts or special tools or supplies needed by the author or illustrator. This often means consumable materials—paper, yarn, paint—items kids would use or make in a hands-on experience as part of the visit.

Extra flip charts might be a big ticket item if an illustrator is doing demonstrations as part of each visit and there are sixteen classrooms on the schedule. It never hurts to anticipate some last minute requests. Some needs may be the result of spontaneous creativity on the part of a particular group.

Equipment

In this day and age, special electronic tools or Internet access or other fairly sophisticated equipment may be needed as part of the visit. Special items may need to be rented or arrangements made to borrow extra slide projectors or other such specialized items. Budget generously if any high-tech equipment is requested. A guest should be asked if any special material or equipment will be needed.

Special Remembrances for Program Attendees

A little reminder of the special visitor are always a nice touch for the special occasion, so you need to budget for some sort of souvenir. Bookmarks designed and autographed by your guest is always a nice token. Posters supplied by the publisher and, if possible autographed, also generate fond memories (see Chapter 2 artwork). A special treat associated with the guest or his/her book is a nice remembrance, like the Mars bar at every place at the tables of the Newbery/Caldecott Banquet the year Jerry Spinelli was honored for *Maniac Magee* (Little, Brown, 1990).

A Small Cushion

This cushion or contingency fund will take care of emergencies or changes in actual costs which come up between the time of your planning and the time of the visit. There's always something, so plan for it.

BOOKS FOR AUTOGRAPHING

A line item may need to be included to account for books ordered and sold for autographing. This item should be self-supporting at the least and can be quite profitable if it is used as a fund raiser. The whole process may be handled separately through the Friends of the Library or the PTO. As the person responsible for all aspects of this visit, keep in mind the need to make arrangements for books written and/or illustrated by your guest.

BUILDING A BUDGET

Hypothetically speaking, let's construct a budget. An author from the New York City area is coming to the Midwest for a one day visit. Program and expenses will be shared by a public library, a school, and a children's literature advocacy group. Check your worksheet!

Worksheet 5-1: Sample Worksheet With Costs

EXPENSES	CONSERVATIVE	MORE REALISTIC
1. HONORARIUM	$800	$1,500
2. TRAVEL	$400 (no Sat. Evening)	$800
3. ROOM	FREE	$69
4. FOOD	$15	$100
5. LOCAL TRANSPORT	$10 (airport and local)	$40
6. MATERIALS	$25	$150
7. EQUIPMENT	NONE	$55 (rental)
8. REMEMBRANCE/TREAT	$30 (4/5 reams paper)	$80 (printing and paper)
9. CONTINGENCY (Cushion)	$25	$25
TOTAL	**$1,305**	**$2,819**

DETAILS ON WHO PAYS FOR WHAT

SHARING THE COSTS

Many budget requests need to be made up to eighteen months before the time of the visit by an author or an illustrator. If requests

---

Worksheet 5-2: Sample Costs

CONSERVATIVE		MORE REALISTIC	
Public Library	**$435**	**Public Library**	**$979**
They initiated visit—responsible for local transportation, materials, etc.		Covered food, room, equipment, and the remembrance.	
School	**$510**	**School**	**$975**
Greatest expense in honoraria for two presentations. Also supported travel expense.		Became responsible for providing the cushion.	
Children's Literature Advocacy Group	**$360**	**Children's Literature Advocacy Group**	**$865**
Funds for honorarium and travel.		Each group shared honorarium and travel plus $10 extra.	
TOTAL	**$1,305**	**TOTAL**	**$2,819**

---

for dollars can accumulate in a special account, it may take two years of requests to acquire the needed money. For example, a Friends of the Library group may budget $1,000 each year for an author visit. If that is the only source of funding, it may take two or three years to build up the necessary funds to meet the expenses.

Be reasonable, but also expect that you will need to spend money to have a quality visit. In the planning stages, ask for adequate funding. If you have money left over, you can always try to negotiate a drop-in or short visit by an unexpected celebrity. Maybe someone is visiting a local bookstore and would be willing to stop by the public library for a short autographing session. Just as important as asking for adequate funds is this advice—Spend what you get!

STRETCHING DOLLARS

- Buy airline tickets well in advance or during price wars to get the lowest fare.

- Arrange for overnight Saturday night to cut costs of airline tickets.

- Share the visit with several libraries or groups so resources can be pooled and expenses shared.

Worksheet 5-3: Blank Worksheet

EXPENSES	CONSERVATIVE	MORE REALISTIC

Cutting Costs

- Use local authors and artists to keep travel expenses contained.

- Piggy-back your visit with other libraries/schools so costs beyond the honorarium can be shared and perhaps held down.

- Use desktop publishing and a copy machine for publicity materials rather than have the expense of an outside printer.

PAYING THE BILLS

Your good reputation comes from paying your bills promptly. One of the easiest ways to handle the expenses associated with an author/illustrator visit is to draw up a purchase order, contract, or appropriate agreement for a stated amount to cover *all* expenses. This includes transportation, room and board, and honorarium. With this agreement guests can take care of his or her own arrangements for travel. A guest may be able to get discounts if he or she gets tickets early or spends more for first class travel if that is important. Obviously, the more frugal he or she is, the greater the amount of their honorarium because that is the amount of money left after their expenses. Many regular travelers like to make their own arrangements because they may link trips to a certain part of the country. Frequent flyer benefits are often desirable for travelers, so your guests will want to have control over their travel plans. Having your contribution set saves you from hassling with another program coordinator over sharing the cost of your leg of the flight or how to split mileage reimbursement.

Purchase Orders

When drawing up one purchase order to cover all expenses make sure you inform your guest of expenses he or she will be expected to pay. When you are making room reservations you should give your guest a choice of hotels, complete with room rates. When you are planning a meal in a restaurant and the author will need to pay for his/her own meal, give an idea of the menu selection and the price range. If there is a local limousine fee, list the cost in your confirming letter. Share taxi rates, subway fares etc., so the visitor can plan accordingly.

It is also a courtesy to include details—for example, *Complimentary continental breakfast with staff on Thursday morning; You will be a dinner guest of the Jones family on Thursday; Lunch on your own on Friday*—when you draw up the daily itinerary. This plan eliminates the hassle of collecting receipts for every activity. You and your guest need to concentrate on providing quality presentations for the audiences involved and the details of keeping receipts and recording mileage can be easily overlooked. Plan time to cover the business aspects of this visit when your guest arrives. This little meeting will just confirm how many matters in particular will be handled. Such a discussion can ease possible tensions.

Try to have a check ready to give to the guest at the end of the presentation or visit. This is an impressive act on your part. It is also reassuring to the artist/writer—No one likes to wait for money!

Working with Friends of the Library groups and school Parent Teacher Organizations often means the check for the guest can be written by the group's treasurer rather efficiently. And, of course, it really is helpful when only *one* check needs to be written.

Be sure you do receive an invoice for the services delivered. Get the invoice beforehand or as you hand over the check. Request an invoice from the presenter before the actual presentation. If this does not happen you may want to have a prepared statement for your guest to sign and date. Provide a space to have their social security number recorded. Check if any other signed documents are required by your library or school.

Proper invoice records keep auditors happy; therefore, your treasurer is happy. Quick and efficient billing keeps you in good

---

Worksheet 5-4: Services Rendered Form

For: Library System or School District

Address

City, State, Zip

Author visit on _____ at _____

TOTAL _____ Signed _____

Name Printed _____ Date _____

Social Security # _____

---

stead with the administrative powers, too. When your request to plan another visit is presented, it will be warmly received in part because of your previous, efficient ways. If you must issue a number of checks, make sure one person is appointed or as designated responsible for the budget. All money matters, ranging from expenses to the collection of funds, must be carefully and closely monitored.

It is wise to have a written set of guidelines available for those persons handling the money. Obtain a signed statement from each group verifying the amount and designated use of their funds. In that way you have a record and a mutual agreement of how to receive and spend the money.

Be prompt in paying your guests if checks cannot be issued immediately after their presentation. This is a common courtesy. Paying all the bills makes it easy to close the account associated with the visit in a timely manner.

Hotels, travel agencies, book publishers—all those businesses, as well as the individuals who contribute to the planning and success of your event will expect a quick turnaround. Plan to deal with your creditors as soon as possible.

Worksheet 5-5: Treasurer's Guidelines

TREASURER GUIDELINES

- Need a copy of budget
- Need copy of contract or letters agreeing to payments and arrangements
- Need a copy of a book order sent (for autographing)
- Need invoices: from the speaker for honorarium; travel
- Agree on selling price for books (be sure to include sales tax)
- Agree that checks to be written for the sale of books be made **Payable to**_____
- Have change for booksellers
- Develop a schedule of booksellers for each event
- Know who is providing transportation and may need reimbursement
- Schedule help to pack and unpack books
- Plan for auxiliary expenses
- Keep an accounting of checks written and the expense they covered

---

TAKING CARE OF DETAILS

You may find that contacting an author/illustrator and contracting for a visit is the easiest part of this job! Again, careful and detailed planning pays off at the actual time of the event.

SPACE

Where will the presentation take place? So often school auditoriums and library meeting rooms are used for presentations by special guests, and in many instances this space may be sterile. It may not take excessive time or energy to create or build some atmosphere in the designated area. For example, you can make welcome banners from bed sheets with a brightly painted message or computer generated banners colored with markers are easily made and posted.

Figure 5-1: Banner Drawn by the Children for Pat Cummings

Murals

You can create murals inspired by the author's works as a pre-visit program or in cooperation with the participating classrooms. Murals can be attached to the walls, bulletin boards, or even hung from the ceiling or light fixtures.

Staging Area

Creating a comfortable stage setting with a sofa or overstuffed chair and a table and lamp will give a homey feeling to a usually bare spot. A special backdrop or a folding screen behind the presenter adds color and interest to the staging area and the backdrop also helps reflect the speaker's voice out toward the audience.

Microphones

Consider the need for a microphone. If an illustrator will be demonstrating drawing technique and facing an easel, a microphone may be needed to assure that children will hear the comments made during the drawing. High ceilings in meeting rooms, auditoriums, and multi-purpose rooms often cause sounds to be lost to the seated audience. Soft-spoken guests definitely need a microphone. After all the planning, it would be a shame to have the visit flop because the audience could not hear. It is a courtesy to consider saving the

Figure 5-2: Display Announcing "Pirate" Visit to Library by Thomas MacGregor

speaker's voice as well. If your guest has been on a week long sojourn of visits and talks, your speaker will appreciate not needing to risk a strained voice.

Cordless, lavaliere microphones are the best. Rent a quality microphone and avoid the possibility of disappointing your audience.

Considering space also means taking into consideration the comfort of the presenter and the audience. This means looking after the creature comforts. Think about the following:

- How long will kids be sitting on the floor?

- Will the room be dark enough for slides to be crisp and sharp?

Figure 5-3: Author George Ella Lyon Is Welcomed to a Setting in Celebration of Her Book *Basket*

Figure 5-4: Children's Librarian Introduces Guest Arnold Adoff to a Dedicated Corner of the Library

- Will everyone be able to hear because most libraries and schools are not outfitted with microphones or speaker systems?

- How long does it take for the energy efficient vapor lights to illuminate the room after they have been turned off? And what will happen in the interim?

- Will the presenter feel as if the children are reaching out to touch them because they are seated so closely or will a big stage put the audience a long distance away?

- Did the sweaty bodies entering the assembly hall just return from recess or field day which is where they would rather be?

- Are the children dragging in their own chairs... a real chore for some, so that this special event is focused more on the weight and difficulty of lugging a chair?

- Did everyone just come from the bookstore or a hands-on workshop so that all audience members are carrying one of those noisy plastic bags so that a low roar of rustling bags will prevail throughout the speaker's talk?

- Are teachers present only because they are required to be with their students?

Worksheet 5-6: Presentation Checklist

PRESENTATION CHECKLIST

- Comfortable setting and seating?
- Microphone?
- Flip chart and markers?
- Table?
- Water and glass?
- Lectern?
- Low stage?
- Slide projector, carousel for slides, and screen?
- Extra projector bulb?
- Extension cord?
- Special equipment/materials: VCR, TV monitor?
- Introduction?

■ Are the adults present to be disciplinarians? Or only to be entertained?

■ Have parents, care-givers, or siblings just dropped off kids at the library, or have teachers seen this break in the schedule as a free time for themselves and left their students in the auditorium?

■ Has a value been placed on this event so that the audience realizes the unique nature of this experience?

THE SUCCESS OF A VISIT

The success of a visit is often measured by the sense of intimacy achieved. Do the people in the audience feel that they have gotten to know this guest? Are they privy to some secret information about the author's personal life or do they now know the funny story behind the naming of a character in the latest book?

In schools, oftentimes the author visit is a culminating event after weeks of reading all the author's books, getting to know the characters, and studying the relationship of the words and the overall impact or meaning of the story as well as the style of illustration and what the pictures bring to the story. An audience so well primed can often be a real challenge for the guest.

In public libraries, in particular, an author's visit may be an introduction to that person and his or her work. The books are displayed and, with luck, all copies are checked out of the library and a long list of reserves is generated.

The difference in these atmospheres may well impact the types of presentation given. When the audience is unfamiliar with a writer, reading aloud creates an enduring memory and a voice to be remembered and heard and felt with the individual's reading of the author's books.

When youngsters have completed a thorough study of an illustrator's works, the guest is usually most comfortable introducing work currently underway. This is a sensible tactic because your guest may have recently worked on this project and the enthusiasm is fresh and sincere. I once heard an illustrator say, *"My favorite book is the one I'm working on right now."*

AUDIENCE QUESTIONS

Questions from the audience are frequently a part of the program. Familiarity with the guest will determine what type of questions are asked. Your guests are often prepared to answer:

How old are you?

Are you rich?

Which book that you have written (or illustrated) is your favorite?

Kids who have read or studied all of your guest's work may ask:

Is the kid in the story you?

Do you spend four hours writing everyday?

How many times did you rewrite this story?

When 300 or more students or people make up the audience for one presentation it might be hard to achieve a sense of "I know you" for each person. Keep this challenge in mind and try to plan for a format or a way to add to this personal involvement of the audience. A receiving line after the presentation may meet this need. With a smaller group, the chance to see the author or illustrator up close while a book is being autographed is another way to achieve this personal bond. A combination of comfort and contact can be key ingredients in the over all impact on individuals of this particular visit.

EQUIPMENT NEEDS

Audio visual equipment is often requested by visiting authors or illustrators. Slide projectors and screens, VCR players, TV monitors, overhead projectors, and flip charts and markers are popular tools for enhancing presentations. Needless to say, all this equipment needs to be checked ahead of time. Make sure you have extra bulbs, extension cords, extra markers or pads of drawing paper on hand for the unexpected moment when the equipment fails.

Someone from the planning committee may need to be designated to work with the guest and be responsible for equipment requests as well as knowing the right moment for turning lights off and equipment on during the presentation.

You cannot hope for a cloudy or rainy day the day of the visit because there is no way to block the sun! Careful planning will also note that shades or drapes need to be pulled ahead of time or blinds must be closed so the level of darkness needed can be met. Sometimes dark paper taped over windows or skylights can achieve the darkness needed. Anticipating that need and resolving the dilemma will add to the day's success. It is an unforgivable error to have slides not clearly visible to the audience.

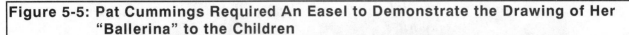

Figure 5-5: Pat Cummings Required An Easel to Demonstrate the Drawing of Her "Ballerina" to the Children

GUARDING AGAINST SURPRISES

Expect some surprises! Hopefully there will be no more than one or two. The best guard is to expect something, and then you will remain cool and common sense will prevail when you must quickly make adjustments or make a statement. Most guests expect to do a good job—their anxiety level may well be as high or higher than yours! With all that nervous energy, things are sure to go well.

Visualize success! In your planning sessions, verbalize the schedule and the order of events—down to the minutes of the day sometimes. This review will be helpful as you must allow time for meals, time for travel and time for traffic jams or road construction, time for long lines of autograph seekers. You will feel more comfortable if you are sure about what is supposed to happen and your confidence will be passed on to your guest.

WHAT FALLS INTO THE UNEXPECTED CATEGORY?

If we knew, it would not be unexpected. But can you see yourself dealing with any or all of the following?

Figure 5-6: Sharing A Book Galley

1. A late plane, bus etc.? Allow a cushion of time for arrival. If possible, have the guest arrive the day or evening before. Everyone will rest better!

2. Lost luggage, notes, slides, or other special equipment? If you are lucky this has already happened to your guest (someplace else!), so they no longer plan to check luggage that holds their tools.

3. A blizzard, hurricane, fog, bad weather? It is best, if this happens, to have it happen at the guest's home driveway or airport because you can often reschedule at no additional fee. If your guest is stranded at your place, cope as best you can, which may mean taking the person into your home. Occa-

Figure 5-7: Addressing A Group of Educators

sionally, the unexpected can have a great impact on your budget. Allow for "disaster" expenses just in case.

4. No one shows up for the program? Oh, this can be so embarrassing and can easily happen someplace like a public library where attending a program is a choice. Sometimes low or no attendance is a reflection on the prior publicity. It can just happen. Be brave, stay upbeat. Do not analyze the disappointment in front of the guest and do not ever blame or even intimate blame on your guest.

5. Keys (or some other important item) are lost, misplaced, or left locked in the car. This may happen to you—not your guest! Guard against this with reasonable precautions. Keep

an extra set of keys in your purse, or desk, or attached to the outside of the car. At any rate, remain calm. This turn of events may prove inconvenient, but solutions are usually within easy reach.

6. Speaker cancels at the last minute? Oftentimes the speaker feels as badly as you do and may work with the publisher or call upon a talented friend to be a substitute. That is a wonderful extension of themselves. This act of cooperation often happens when sickness or an unexpected emergency occurs.

It is no secret that a fast approaching deadline for an editor may cause a last minute panic and cause an unapologetic cancellation. There is often little you can do. Be consoled that the word gets around about authors or artists who are unreliable and other invitations are often withheld.

Sometimes a way to guard against a last minute cancellation is to schedule a series of paid presentations—perhaps stops in two or three locations within your area in a week—so a fairly substantial amount of money is involved. To cancel several appearances or several days of bookings will definitely have a financial impact. The guest may then be more reluctant to cancel at the last minute. However, remember these talented people have commitments and important deadlines which loom over their heads just as your own priorities do. To all of them, the key to their continuing success is completing books. Therefore, doing what is necessary to reach that end is always a top priority.

All decisions on how to cope with last minute changes do not need to be yours alone. That is part of the reason for having a planning committee. All of them can be available to share the burden and wisdom of the decision. Your guest may also offer a solution because they have been involved in other delays or last minute changes. This participation on their part can be helpful.

TIME LINE

It is not a sign of your age, it is a sign of the times that the days, weeks, and months seem to fly by! A timeline will serve as a reminder of where you and your committee's work should be at critical times. Give yourself plenty of time. There is *no substitute* for plenty of time for planning.

Murphy's Law exists for all of us, so plan that no phone call will get through on the first try and that your other responsibilities will distract you someplace in the planning process. Realistically, popular and well-known authors and illustrators are booked months, often years, in advance or you may need to make plans early because you need to organize a fund-raiser. It is also true that it is not easy to get 100 copies of an author's book on short notice nor does it take just one phone call to organize a Friends group to act as hosts for your autographing session.

Everyone will more likely remain calm (and good friends) if adequate lead-time exists. Naturally, special events or designated awareness periods like November's National Children's Book Week, libraries' National Library Week, and the school's favorite Right-to-Read Week, and Black History Month, can make for logical times to spotlight an author or illustrator. But, because these are national celebrations many other people may share your desire to have an author or an illustrator as their special guest. Contacting publishers early will get you in the queue and the publisher may do much of the planning and decision-making for you by trying to squeeze in as many stops as possible on a promotional tour.

A time line will force you to focus your plans so no detail is overlooked. A successful planner often delegates many of the responsibilities, so following up to be sure everyone is having success, is all that is needed. A typical time line might look like this:

12-18 months: Accept the challenge or begin the brainstorming process for choosing a guest or meeting a goal to have an author or illustrator visit—publishers' catalogs list the states where authors and illustrators live. You may find great talent, of which you were not aware, locally.

9-12 months: Contact a publisher for a list of possible speakers, information on the costs involved, projections on new books, and their promotion plans. At this point it may be better to build coalitions and assure the necessary funds.

8 months: Make a choice and confirm in writing the initial plan, promising to follow-up with more details as the time gets closer. It's good to send copies of your correspondence to the author/illustrator, the publisher, all members of your planning committee, and your supervisor. Too much communication is better than not enough.

3-4 months: If a school, for example, will be featuring all the works of a special guest, long term writing projects or art projects may supplement the visit so curriculum plans will need to be adjusted accordingly.

3-4 months: Work with the publisher, a jobber, or a local bookstore on the availability of the guest's books. Select titles to be ordered or sent on consignment. A written follow-up is always good at this point. Many publishing houses send books for autographing regularly and have an efficient system—including excellent discounts—already in place. You will need a statement or contract verifying the titles, format (hardback or paperback and perhaps CD) and numbers of each title you plan to have available.

Depending on your guest and the number of books they have written, or the number of titles you want to offer for sale, you may need to request books from more than one publisher. Also, you might want to ask the publisher if they can provide bookplates for the author to autograph, just in case the full order does not arrive, or you run short of books to sign.

2 months: This is also a good time to carefully plan what will happen during the guest's visit. Developing an itinerary means coordinating the daily schedules of many people, so this step can be very time consuming. It is also none too soon to start getting the word out to the students and/or the public about the approaching visit.

Worksheet 5-7: Time Line Outline

12-18 months ahead	Begin planning: expect the need for a long lead time if you are expecting a prominent author or illustrator.
9-12 months ahead	contact publisher
8-9 months ahead	plan program
6-8 months ahead	confirm visit, program, costs, sites; make arrangements for travel and housing plan publicity
3-4 months ahead	order books for selling and autographing
Two months ahead	develop detailed itinerary; begin local publicity
One month ahead	confirm arrangements with all sites; finalize details
Two weeks ahead	confirmation call to the author or illustrator; check for any last minute adjustments
One week ahead	confirm local arrangements; distribute final itinerary
Day before	check on room set-up arrangements; remind drivers, hosts, newspaper etc.; familiarize yourself with all of the details
Few days later	send out follow-up publicity; hold evaluation meeting; write thank you notes
Six weeks after	return unsold books; pay all bills; celebrate and dream of next author or illustrator visit

6 IMPORTANCE OF CORRESPONDENCE

When visits are a collaborative effort, many schedules need to be meshed and all lines of communication need to be open. Just because this planned author/illustrator visit is one of the highlights of your program planning year, and it is important to you, that may not be true for your peers and colleagues.

When many people are involved, it is difficult to keep all parties equally informed if you rely solely on verbal communication. This dilemma can be alleviated by planning to capture the progress and changes in writing and dispense that in a timely manner. It is disappointing to hear about changes in a conference speaker from the bookstore manager when you are on the planning/advisory committee!

It is also a good idea to communicate the status quo if you have not worked with your committee for several weeks or if you all are in different buildings, agencies, or even towns. You will get burned if you constantly follow the adage no news is good news.

It is particularly important that correspondence with your guest be timely and as complete as possible. Being able to update and add detail to a letter that you have already sent will keep all the information together. It is always good to keep the approaching visit in the author's mind (and on his/her calendar, too.!)

For example, when the program time changes from 2 P.M. to 1 P.M., reformat the original letter and include the whole paragraph so the change clearly reflects the plans for the whole day rather than dashing off a note which says, *Thursday's program is now at 1 P.M., rather than 2 P.M.* A designation that this is a revised schedule, or whatever, will keep all the information handy and orderly for you and your guest.

SAMPLE LETTERS

The following letters are sample correspondence with visiting authors to let them know what their schedule will be like when they visit.

Figure 6-1: Letter to Pat Cummings

Wood County District Public Library ● 251 N. Main St. ● Bowling Green, OH 43402-2477
Telephone: 419/352-5104 ● FAX: 419/354-0405

September 15 1992

Pat Cummings

Brooklyn, N.Y 11231

Dear Pat:

Welcome home! Hope your trip was safe, successful and satisfying. And for those of us who look forward to your new work—inspiring!

I promised you a blow-by-blow account of your schedule when you visit Northwest Ohio—so here goes...

This whole idea is the product of CSCL (Cooperative Services for Children's Literature), a group of educators and librarians affiliated with Bowling Green State University's Jerome Library. Our goal is to support educators in our area who are interested in children's literature. Each fall we sponsor a Book and Reader Conference with mini-workshops, books, dinner, and a special author/illustrator guest.

In order to "spread the joy of a celebrity in town," we arrange visits to schools and/or libraries.

Thursday, October 1:

      Arrival at Toledo Express Airport

           11:15 am (you'll be met by Bonnie Chambers, newly semi-retired education professor from BGSU and

      chairperson of CSCL)

Bonnie will welcome you and chauffeur you to Bowling Green—where, with luck, I might be able to meet you for a quick lunch before you make your first school visit at...

      Crim Elementary School

           Beth Johnson, principal

           Deb Hoover, school librarian

                 1:30-2:00 or so

                      Grades 1-3. Approximately 150 kids (microphone, flip chart, and markers available).

                 2:30-3:10 or so

                      Grades 4-6. Approximately 180 kids (microphone, flip chart, and markers available).

Both groups would love an "illustrated" talk—that chance to see you "work" and I'm sure the older kids would like to know about your career choices and how you ended up writing as well as illustrating childrens books. We might schedule a short autographing session after the second group for youngsters who purchased your books at the school book fair the week before.

The CSLS Book and Reader conference is from 4-8 pm. You will have some time to freshen up before you arrive in Perrysburg for that. A box supper will be served at 6:15 pm., followed by your talk at 7:00 pm or so. (I'd expect you'll arrive between 5:00 and 5:30 pm, and you may be asked to autograph your books. A local children's bookstore owner will be selling books before supper as well as after your talk).

Bonnie will have some announcements and appropriate news about CSCL at 7:00 pm and then I'll introduce you. We can expect 150 (or more we hope!), mostly teachers, so the love of story, etc. is always a good topic—but I think again many would be interested in your "becoming a writer of children's books." Of course, "secrets" about what you're working on now are always relished! I can't imagine you won't have some exciting adventures of your Ghana trip to relate. So...the 40 or so minutes shall pass quickly.

One of our local Bowling Green motels will host you overnight—promising rest and rejuvenation because Friday's another day—and a busy one at that!

Figure 6-1: Continued

Friday, October 2:

    Starr School

      Marti Smock, principal

Again, Bonnie will drive you to the Toledo suburb of Oregon. The two presentations will be similar to the ones at Crim.

      9:30-10:00 am or so

        Grades K-2. Approximately 300 kids (microphone, flip chart, and markers available).

      10:30-11:10 am or so

        Grades 3-6. Approximately 335 kids (microphone, flip chart, and markers available).

Autographing at this school will be limited.

Then a tour of Interstate 75 begins! Bonnie will escort you to Findlay, Ohio, with lunch along the way (you'll actually stop—I don't think you'll need to eat in the car!).

    Findlay High School

      Vicki Hardesty, school librarian. She'll be at the Book and Reader Conference Thursday evening, so it'll be like meeting an old (18 hours at least!) friend.

      1:30-2:15 pm

        880-100 high school art students

This is probably a "career pep talk," and I bet they'd enjoy a "drawing demonstration" too. You had mentioned the possibility of using slides, so Vicki will have a carousel projector and screen available.

Your return flight is from Toledo at 5:00 pm to Cleveland and then on to a real plane to La Guardia.

Hope this meets your expectations. Let me know if there's any special equipment you might need or if you would like to use slides at any other presentations. We'll do our best!

I know these trips can be tiring for you, but they are such an inspiration to teachers and such a thrill for children. And I say, "Whatever it takes to make them readers and lovers of books," — do it!

Can't wait to see you

Fondly,

Kathy East

P.S. Any chance you could "whip up"—or maybe you have a standard camera-ready bookmark with your autograph? If you'd FAX me such a thing, we could produce bookmarks as a token of your visit. (It also cuts down on the number of requests for your autograph on odd bits of paper). It would be a nice way to make the link between the author/illustrator and the book.

P.P.S. Enclosed are your airline tickets!

    Walbridge Branch Library   Bradner Branch Library
    108 North Main   130 North Main
    Walbridge, OH 43465   Bradner, OH 43406
    419/666-9900

Figure 6-2: Letter to Arnold Adoff

Wood County District Public Library ● 251 N. Main St. ● Bowling Green, OH 43402-2477
Telephone: 419/352-5104 ● FAX: 419/354-0405

August 1, 1989

Mr. Arnold Adoff

Yellow Springs, Ohio 45387

Dear Arnold:

It was so nice to see you at ALA! And even better to hear your confirmation of the visit to northwest Ohio.

Melissa Cain is the University of Toledo contact for the evening presentation to teachers and librarians. She and I have talked and we're both willing to organize your life for that day!

So here it goes—

the day is Thursday, September 28th.

—an early afternoon visit with 8th graders at the Bowling Green Junior High (probably 100 kids per session) probably 2 sessions; thought you might like to do the Christopher Columbus bookmark story—it's so real! And a bit of reading of poetry. Is 45 minutes per session enough time? Then we'd like an autograph session. The school librarian, Elaine Ezell, will sell books earlier in the week, so we'll know how many. We're hoping to get the Sweet Dreams bookmark from Lothrop so everyone will have your autograph—so we can avoid autographing those little odd scraps of paper.

Then,

a family program at the Wood County Public Library (that's my stomping ground!) Again, I think about 45 minutes. I'd like you to do lots of Chocolate Dreams. This chocoholic would be in seventh heaven! I hope to arrange a chocolate treat for the audience. Our Friends of the Library will sell books for autographing at the library .

And then—

off to Perrysburg High School for the Cooperative Services for Children's Literature workshop. That's dinner, SPEECH and more autographing.

Really, in this one visit, all of northwest Ohio will love you—if they don't t already.

I didn't look into bus schedules to Bowling Green from Dayton and/or Columbus but I'd gladly do that. If the bus doesn't work out, I could probably work out a way to pick you up, etc.

The children's bookstore, Once upon a Mind, in Maumee is ordering books for all of these occasions, but could you supply us with photos of you for our promotional bulletin boards, etc (at least 4).

The school and library will together pay $500 am CSCL will take care of the evening honorarium and expenses. Is that your understanding?

In brief:

Thursday, September 28th

Figure 6-2: Continued

Arrive Bowling Green

12:30-	presentation at Bowling Green Junior High Contact: Elaine Ezell (419) 354-0200
12:30-1:15	half 8th graders
1:30-2:15	other half 8th graders (in auditorium)
2:15-2:45	Autographing (school media center)
BREAK	
4:00-4:45	Family Program at Wood County Public Library, 251 North Main, Contact: Kathy East (419) 352-5104
4::45-5:15	Autographing
5:15-5:45	Travel to Perrysburg
6:00-10:00	CSCL program, dinner & workshops

End of a Wonderful Day!

Melissa and the CSCL group will make arrangements for you to stay overnight.

No doubt all this planning has raised some questions, so feel free to call or write.

Enjoy what's left of summer... and rest up for your visit.

My best to Virginia!

Fondly,

Kathy East

cc: E. Ezell

   M. Cain

P.S. I ordered <u>Chocolate Dreams</u>, <u>Sports Pages</u>, <u>All the Colors of the Race</u>, and <u>Greens</u> for the school visit. Should I have some copies of <u>Eats</u> too?

   For the library, I ordered <u>Chocolate Dreams</u>.

Walbridge Branch Library	Bradner Branch Library
108 North Main	130 North Main
Walbridge, OH 43465	Bradner, OH 43406
419/666-9900	419/288-2442

Figure 6-3: Letter to Thomas Scheidt

Wood County District Public Library ● 251 N. Main St. ● Bowling Green, OH 43402-2477
Telephone: 419/352-5104 ● FAX: 419/354-0405

September 15, 1992

Mr. Thomas Scheidt

Time Machine Productions

Dayton, OH 45429

Dear Thomas:

We're all looking forward to your visit to Wood County in October as Thomas MacGregor! What the Black Swamp needs is an authentic pirate full of story, song, and music.

Here's the schedule as I see it:

Friday, October 9th:

1:30 p.m.	Wood County District Public Library
	251 North Main St., Bowling Green
	419/352-5104

We've invited the 5th grade classes from our local schools (8 schools, although all may not attend...and that's good—they may not all fit!)

4 p.m. Same place

A public performance, all ages.

7:30 p.m.	Weston Public Library
	Main & Locust Streets, Weston
	419/669-3415
	contact person: Mary Fellows

Public performance, all ages.

Dennis and I would happily house you and whomever assists you at our home in Perryburg on Friday night (hope you're not allergic to Brittany Spaniels, we have two—also a teenage son!)

Figure 6-3: Continued

Saturday, October 10th schedule:

    11a.m.. Rossgord Public Library

          720 Dixie Hwy, Rossford

          419/666-0924

          contact person: Mike French/Mary Mura

Public performance, all ages.

    1:30 p.m.   Way Public Library

          101 E. Indiana Ave., Perrysburg

          419/874-3135

          contact person: Nancy Kelley/Peggy Pile

Public performance, school-age and up.

I've included a county map and a kind of "trip tic" for your journeys. If this is a false sense of security, our staff will gladly help you out. Of course, that assumes you'll get to Bowling Green—but you're experienced!

Do you have a black & white photo you could send? I'd do a press release and schedule for the paper and the photo would be a nice enhancement.

We have some of the summer reading program packets you supplied which I can give each library to use for their own publicity.

Each of the library's will assume the cost of their performance(s) and will have a $175 check for each performance for you that day. However, you will need to provide an invoice for each library. Could you mail that invoice ahead of time? (Or mail them all to me and I'll gladly distribute them.) Have I forgotten anything?

We know you provide your own PA system and perform for crowds of 6 to 600 or more... you need a table to set up display items and if possible a way to hang a flag or something, right?

Keep in touch...in good voice...etc. Thank you for working with all of the libraries.

Sincerely,

Kathy East

Asst. Director/Head of Children's Services

cc: Weston

       Way

       Rossford

        Walbridge Branch Library   Bradner Branch Library

        108 North Main   130 North Main

        Walbridge, OH 43465   Bradner, OH 43406

        419/666-9900   419/288-2442

Figure 6-4: Letter to Lee Bennett Hopkins

Wood County District Public Library ● 251 N. Main St. ● Bowling Green, OH 43402-2477
Telephone: 419/352-5104 ● FAX: 419/354-0405

May 17, 1991

Mr. Lee Bennett Hopkins
Scarborough, NY 10510

Dear Lee Bennett Hopkins:

Guess you're coming to visit and we've got lots of people looking forward to seeing you!

This note is to confirm plans made with Hughes Moir earlier this spring to visit Northwest Ohio.

I envision your schedule going something like this:

Thursday, September 19th:

> You arrive at Toledo Express Airport some time before noon.

> You will be met and escorted to Bowling Green.

Thursday afternoon:

> Visit to Conneaut School. Grades 1-3 session, 45 minute session. Grades 4-6 session, 45 minute session. This school has pledged to start off the '91 school year with a poetry unit. Everything here is integrated—reading, listening, the arts and writing. The teachers and children love special guests and honor them with enthusiasm and respect.

> No doubt an autograph session will be requested! (Could you send your autograph ahead of time and I could make a bookmark for kids who aren't purchasing books but will be excited to have had you at their school?)

After school Thursday:

We could hold an open family program at the public library. Perhaps a half-hour or so of "getting to know you" and for you to read poems.

The CSCL (Cooperative Services for Children's Literature) program is Thursday evening. Teachers and librarians gather for small discussion groups, a light supper and a guest—You! That's 40-45 minutes of sharing and then autographing. A local children's bookstore has usually assisted so books will be available.

On Friday morning we would like you to visit two gifted classes (probably 20 students each) in the Perrysburg schools.

Figure 6-4: Continued

I know this sounds like a full schedule, and it is. . .but your visit is a special treat and we want to allow a variety of youngsters and teachers to get to know you.

It's our understanding that your costs are $1000 honorarium and expenses. If you would make the flight arrangements, we'll take care of food, accommodations and transportation to and from the airport.

Could you also put us in contact with your publicist? Pictures and "books for sale" are a must!

Feel free to contact me if you have questions about these arrangements or just need someone to talk to!

Looking forward to your visit and to working with you! Is there a chance I might see you at ALA in Atlanta?

Sincerely,

Kathy East

Asst. Director &

Head of Children's Services

P.S. Thanks so much for saying "yes" to Hughes' invitation! You said it best, <u>Good Books, Good Times</u>!

Walbridge Branch Library	Bradner Branch Library
108 North Main	130 North Main
Walbridge, OH 43465	Bradner, OH 43406
419/666-9900	

Figure 6-5: Letter to Seymour Simon

PUBLIC LIBRARY of COLUMBUS and FRANKLIN COUNTY
28 SOUTH HAMILTON RD.
COLUMBUS, OHIO 43213

December 14, 1987

Dear Mr. Simon:

It's really exciting to think you are willing to add Columbus to your tour of Ohio in May of '88.

The Public Library of Columbus and Franklin County has received special funds in 1987 to add science materials to the collection. The children's librarians concentrated on resources for science fair projects as our community schools seem to involve students in this activity from September to June.

Our plan (should you choose to accept it) is to gather 100 or so eighth graders at our South High Branch to visit with you and hopefully get your perspective on "the student as scientist." Incorporating materials from your books on optical illusions, the night sky, planets and space would really spark their interest and curiosity. A display in the library would feature science fair projects from schools in the branch's service area.

If you could fly to Columbus on Thursday, May 12 (later afternoon or early evening) we would put you up in a hotel overnight. Friday morning's program would start at 9:30 A.M. or so and last about an hour. We would like to have some paperback copies of your books available for sale and autographs. Everything should be finished by noon to allow time for lunch and the drive to Shaker Heights (someone from our staff will chauffeur you).

Of course, we are open to suggestions if there is something else you would rather present. Just let me know.

I hope all of this makes sense and is amenable! I expect your honorarium to be _____ and the library will pay your hotel and meal expenses. A portion of the airfare is also negotiable. Before any of this can be finalized I'll need your reactions <u>and</u> your social security number.

With the holiday season and lots of days away from the office, perhaps we can talk on the phone in January. Or if you would rather write—I'd love to get your autograph!

Sincerely,

Kathy East

Coordinator of Children and Young Adult Services

cc: A. Davis

    E. Stephanian

KE:gg

7 PUBLICIZING/ADVERTISING THE VISIT

In many cases, all of your hard work will pay off only if you have an audience. Even dealing with schools where you believe you have a captive audience (at least if the visit is held during school hours) it is important for faculty and parents to be informed and become enthusiastic. Parental support means name recognition of the guest, dollars to purchase copies of the featured books, and genuine discussion of the importance of books and reading and the talents of the people able to write and illustrate children's and young adults' materials.

Don't hesitate to ask publishers for free materials to be used as part of your publicity plan. Often publishers can supply a box of posters, bookmarks, stickers, buttons, photographs, biographical information, bibliographies, and occasionally free copies of the books written and/or illustrated by your intended guest speaker. They may also send you the galleys for the newest title. Because many promotional materials are put together each year for free distribution at various library and booksellers conferences, take whatever the publisher offers—it is free and program attendees love to get mementoes related to the speaker or his/her books.

LOCAL PUBLICITY

To build anticipation for up-coming events, the word must get out. Posters are usually an easy and wise method to relay the most important message—something special is coming. It is important that people know that they should reserve a particular date, day, and time.

Internally generated posters, put up in the library, will inform members of the public who regularly visits your library. However, to broaden the potential audience posters should be taken to other places as well. Public libraries can often post information in school buildings and school libraries. Don't forget day care and community centers, shopping malls, and places like the laundromat. Many restaurants and business establishments have community bulletin boards or allow the placing of posters in their windows or in vestibules.

Request photos from the publishers because posters featuring a picture of your guest will attract a second look. Sophisticated copy machines and computer scanners can produce a clear likeness from a photo, too. Plan to use photographs and eye-catching graphics and typeface to enhance your posters. Half-page handouts or a quantity of bookmarks are wise publicity items.

Figure 7-1: Flyer Advertising a Visit From Wendy Parker, Author of *The Christmas Doll*

The Christmas Doll

From Pencil to Print

an exhibit of how a book is created by Columbus author and artist

WENDY PARKER

**Now through December1
at the Main Library of the Public Library
of Columbus and Franklin County
96 South Grant Avenue**

Wendy Mathis Parker's delightful Christmas story in verse and illustration is traced from pencil to publisher's print at the Main Library's New Gallery for both young and old to see how a book is created and to enjoy her creative watercolors. If the scenes in her illustrations happen to resemble the neighborhoods of German Village, it is no coincidence.

**Meet the author/artist on
December 1 at 11 a.m.**
Make your own Christmas Doll and meet the author/artist at the Main Library. You just might persuade her to autograph your copy of THE CHRISTMAS DOLL, published by Holt-Reinhardt, while the youngsters enjoy a Christmas crafts session.

Figure 7-2: Flyer with Author Jackie Torrence's Picture with Story-Time Information

JACKIE TORRENCE
nationally   acclaimed
as the
STORY LADY

Enjoy a special
story-telling treat
for the whole family.

Friday   evening
May 4, 1990
7:00 P.M.*

Wood County District Public Library
251 North Main
Bowling Green, OH 43402

FREE tickets available at the library
or call 352-5104.

*The library will open especially for this event;
no other library services will be available.

Library patrons, children in schools, and others can carry bookmarks and flyers home and be reminded of the details—who, what, where, and when (see Chapter 3). Bookmarks have space on the back to list the author or illustrator's books (see Chapter 2). Your potential audience may want to check out the books done by your up-coming guest. Create a display (see Chapter 5). Having enough copies of the books can be very critical to the publicity plan. Consider limiting the books' circulation to just one week for about six weeks before and two weeks after the visit.

Press releases to newspapers and PSAs (public service announcements) to local radio and television stations are practical ways to get the word out about the upcoming visit.

After the press releases are sent, a follow-up call can offer an interview with your guest. If time permits, a live broadcast on a call-in radio show can be a very special event. Inviting the media to one of the presentations can help assure local coverage.

Newspaper Coverage

Expect a big response when the newspaper runs a picture with the program announcement. The paper's readership notices the picture

Figure 7-3: Flyer with Author Lee Bennett Hopkins' Picture with a Brief Biography

Lee Bennett Hopkins

VISITS

CONNEAUT SCHOOL

FRIDAY, SEPTEMBER 20

Lee Bennett Hopkins is a poet and an anthologist, which means he likes to collect the poems of many different authors and make a book of poems on a specific topic like creatures, dinosaurs and good books! Mr. Hopkins has taught elementary school students, served as a visiting professor at colleges and universities and worked as a consultant. His enthusiasm for the rhythms and rhymes of words makes him a wonderful guest to encourage youngsters to listen, sing and write lots and lots of words.

Figure 7-4: Press Release Announcing Author Lee Bennet Hopkins' Visit

Wood County District Public Library ● 251 N. Main St. ● Bowling Green, OH 43402-2477
Telephone: 419/352-5104 ● FAX: 419/354-0405

September 11, 1991

The Daily Sentinel-Tribune
300 East Poe Road
Bowling Green, OH 43402

FOR IMMEDIATE RELEASE:

Author to Visit Bowling Green

Author-anthologist Lee Bennett Hopkins will be in Bowling Green for several events next Thursday and Friday. Hopkins is a poet, writer and popular speaker at meetings and conferences. The underlying theme of his work is a dedication to bringing books and children together. "You must teach children to love books," he insists. "We spend too much time teaching children to read, and not enough time teaching them to love to read."

His first presentation will be a program for families at the Wood County District Public Library, 251 North Main Street at 4 P.M. on Thursday. He'll share poems from several of the anthologies to his credit. To Mr. Hopkins that means bringing an "ooh" feeling to the listeners. Some of his books will be available for purchase and autographing. His visit is supported by the Friends of the Wood County Library and the William Halferty memorial.

Walbridge Branch Library
108 North Main
Walbridge, OH 43465
419/666-9900

Bradner Branch Library
130 North Main
Bradner, OH 43406

and are reminded that tomorrow is the author visit. Or send a copy of the guest's latest book to the editor. This may generate a phone interview before the planned arrival. Sometimes good publicity through many sources before the event may mean the press will not carry a picture of the event—or even carry a follow-up story. Invite a reporter.

If possible, take pictures during the event and send them to the local papers for a follow-up story. This tactic is often very satisfying to community funders when the follow-up story mentions their names. Make sure that you or someone on staff is familiar with the policies and practices of your local newspaper and work with the editor to obtain the most meaningful coverage.

Public Service Announcements—PSAs

Free PSAs (public service announcements) are available only on educational television within the local community. However, with PSAs you may reach an audience that does not read the paper daily. Past experience has seen some library PSAs played at 11:30 P.M. or dawn, not exactly prime time for children to see or be attracted to your library program. Monitor your local station. Do not be afraid to ask for play during regular programming for kids.

Figure 7-5: Follow-Up Newspaper Coverage for Author/Illustrator Pat Cummings *(reprinted with permission by Sentinal-Tribune, Bowling Green, OH; Copyright 1993)*

Author describes her work to Crim students

By MARTIN IACAMPO JR.
BG PR Intern

Children's book author and illustrator Pat Cummings spoke to the students of Crim Elementary School Thursday.

As she stood before the children with her books behind her, she told them about her life and her career as an author and illustrator. She told them that the first thing she ever drew was a scribble, and then she colored in the scribble with her huge box of crayons.

Ms. Cummings' explained that her first recognizable drawing was a result of a childhood experience she had while living in Germany. One day she was outside playing with her older sister, Linda. When Linda went inside, Ms. Cummings became bored and got on a bus that had stopped to let some people off. The bus took her and some German girls to a ballet school where it was discovered she didn't belong.

She got sent home and landed in a lot of trouble. "I was grounded for about 20 years," Ms. Cummings recalled. Because she had a lot of time on her hands,'she began to draw ballerinas, which she would then sell at school for a nickel, a Twinkie, or some M&Ms.

She attended Pratt, an art institute, where she earned a bachelor's degree in fine arts. She began her career as an illustrator by working with a children's theater group.

Upon graduation, she only illustrated children's books, but later realized she could do more illustrating if she wrote the books herself.

Some of the books Ms. Cummings has written and illustrated include "Jimmy Lee Did It," "C.L.O.U.D.S.," and "Clean Your Room, Harvey Moon."

Photo by Mark Deckard

Author and illustrator Pat Cummings visited Crim Elementary School Thursday afternoon to discuss her approach to writing children's books.

During her presentation, Ms. Cummings also showed the students the steps she goes through to write, illustrate and prepare a rough copy of a book. She told them that a final copy of a book starts out as a poster with all the pages printed on one huge sheet of paper. The poster is then cut up and bound so it looks like a book, she explained.

Ms. Cummings suggested the students practice if they want to improve on some skill or interest they may have. When one student asked her how she got to draw so well, she replied, "If you like drawing, you draw more and more."

Ms. Cummings' visit was a cooperative effort between the Crim P.T.O, Bowling Green State University, and the Wood County Public Library. The visit has been planned for over a year.

The children had been preparing for the visit for several weeks. They read several of her books, discussed the stories, and did activities related to the themes.

Fourth-grade students also created a poster with ballerinas on it for one of their projects prior to Ms. Cummings' visit and gave the poster to the author as a gift.

8 PLANNING FOR AUTOGRAPHING

One of the most enchanting rituals connected with being in the presence of an author or an illustrator is to get an autograph. What a luxury to have the undivided attention of this famous person as your own name is inscribed in the book! This ritual can be very time consuming and frustrating, if not handled well.

First, adequate copies of your guest's book or books need to be on hand. Publishers are very helpful in advising you on how to request books. Ordering directly from the publisher usually means the price of the book will have a worthwhile discount. However, you should expect to pay the shipping costs. If your library works with a children's book jobber, ask if the jobber has a program for supplying books for celebrity visits. Because you are a regular customer, you may not need to pay shipping costs.

The most difficult job is guessing how many books to order. Obviously, the newest book has the greatest appeal but with prolific authors/illustrators, choosing from a multitude of titles may be more difficult. If the author tells you which book or books will be featured in his or her talk, you can bet that book will be most popular for purchase.

The cost of the book will have an impact on the number of books you sell. A hardback book becomes the new book autographed for the whole family to cherish. It's unusual to have families purchase several hardback books if the cost is $12-15 for each book. If paperback editions are available, they will sell best. Each child in a family will more likely be able to choose a title to own.

The season of your visit may also help buyers decide what to purchase. The approaching holiday season may encourage buying autographed books as gifts. You can always plant the idea that autographed books make wonderful gifts in general, so that grandparents and others may think of upcoming birthdays and special events which may be remembered appropriately with a book.

Learn the habits of your community. How much do they value books? How much money might they spend on books? Publicity should make program attendees aware that books will be available for purchase and autographing. Listing approximate prices will help people plan their purchases.

If your patrons are used to buying books at the library at book sale prices, they may be very surprised at the cost of *new* books. However, a good speaker and a friendly atmosphere will generate good sales. If the price is reduced (taking into account the publisher's discount) to below what the bookstore sells the book for . . .

you have an attractive product. Be sure to advertise the fact that a discount is being provided. If the profits of the book sales will benefit a special cause be sure the audience is made aware of this. Purchasers like to know they will acquire a personally autographed book *and* benefit the Friends group or the PTO.

The actual selling of the books needs to be handled by the PTO, the Mother's Club, The Friends of the Library, or a similar group. Be sure state sales tax laws are met.

SELLING BOOKS

It is important to take care with the new books sent by the publisher. They need to be kept in a safe place so a careful inventory can be maintained. You need to return all unsold books (in excellent condition) and pay for the remainder. When books sell for different prices it is very confusing, especially if sales are brisk. Take care with the cash box! One person from the planning committee should be in charge of all currency—checks, cash, charges (if applicable).

Early on, the philosophy needs to be adopted that we only have the money we have. Driving yourself to distraction keeping track of every penny is wasted energy. Encourage buyers to purchase by check. It is the safest method and eliminates errors in making change as well as takes away the temptations brought on when cash is around. Stamp the back of the checks immediately with *"for deposit only."*

If selling extends over several hours or days, be sure to plan for a frequent pick-up of large bills and checks. Be sure money is deposited or put in a safe. Schools may ask classroom teachers or an aide or parent volunteer to coordinate the ordering and payment of books for each grade or classroom. All monies need to be closely accounted for and should be handled carefully.

DISPLAYING THE BOOKS

Depending on how many books you have on hand and how many different titles will be available, make an attractive display of the books for sale. Put out signs clearly listing each book title and the selling price (tax included.)

Another sign should tell how to make out checks. Have the sign read:

Make checks payable to _____

Figure 8-1: Sample Order Form

Student's

Name_____

Teacher's Name_____

Books are for sale and youngsters may have their book autographed.

TITLES AVAILABLE	# OF COPES	PRICE
Best Friends. Eighteen poems celebrating the fun of being friends (K3). Hardback.	_____ @ $12.89	_____
Click. Rumble. Roar. Poems about car washes, power shovels, the laundromat and other machines. Grades 26. Hardback.	_____ @ $13.89	_____
Creatures. English and American poems featuring magical and supernatural creatures. All ages, paperback.	_____ @ $3.95	_____
Dinosaurs. Just what you always wanted— rhymes about dinosaurs! All ages, paperback.	_____ @ $4.95	_____
Good Books. Good Times! Poems on the joys of reading—the title poem written by Hopkins himself. All ages, hardback.	_____ @ $12.95	_____
More Surprises. Poems grouped in sections labeled "Body Parts," "Living Things," "Hot and Cold," etc. (I Can Read Book, paperback)	_____ @ $3.50	_____

Total # Books _____ Total $ _____

Return this order to school as soon as possible!

Make checks payable to: **FRIENDS OF THE WOOD COUNTY LIBRARY**

*Books are available on a first come, first served basis, as long as the supply of books holds out!

****

Message for autograph:

Student's Name:_____Teacher's Name_____

Worksheet 8-1: Blank Order form

BOOK ORDER FORM

(Insert School Name)

Student's Name _____

Teacher's Name _____

Books are for sale and youngsters may have their book autographed.

TITLES AVAILABLE	# OF COPIES	PRICE

Total # Books_____Total $_____

Return this order to school as soon as possible!

Make checks payable to:

(Insert School or Organization Name Here)

*Books are available on a first come, first served basis, as long as the supply of books holds out.

_____

Message for Autograph:

_____

_____

_____

Student's Name_____Teacher's Name_____

You need one person to keep the books in order and the supply replenished. Another person can calculate the total charge for the sale, take money or checks, make change, and give or offer receipts. (Most groups do not have the ability to accept charge cards, but if you work cooperatively with a bookstore, using credit cards may be fine.)

PURCHASING THE BOOKS

If the number of books that can be purchased is to be limited, make sure a sign is posted ahead of time. Is buying limited to only one copy of each title? Or can only one book per person be purchased and autographed? Limiting sales and/or the number of books which may be autographed will impact the number of books sold. Publicity ahead of time might make note of the purchasing limitations. The amount of time allotted in the schedule for autographing impacts the planning committee's decision on limitations.

If selling many copies of your guest's books is an important part of the fund-raising efforts, then be sure to allow adequate time for the autographing activity. Schools often limit students' purchasing to one book for autographing, but even if most students bought only one book, in many schools, that means sales of 250 or more books!

Remember that many authors and illustrators expect their library and school visits to generate additional sales of their books. If you have talked with a publisher's representative, you may get some idea of how much of an issue the sale of books might be!

If you would rather not be responsible for ordering and selling books, an alternative suggestion is to work with a local bookstore. Let the store order and sell books. Ask for a percentage of the sales to benefit your institution. Bookstores which run or attend school book fairs are used to this arrangement and if you are expecting a big crowd or the author/illustrator is visiting several schools this choice can be a workable alternative. You will need to work together in making an educated guess of how many copies of individual titles need to be ordered. Add someone from the bookstore to your planning committee if you choose to have the bookstore handle book sales. The details for the autographing events may then need to be adjusted.

BOOK SALES PROFITS

Profits from the sales of books may help to defray some of your expenses. Depending on the number of children your author will see and the cost of the books your audience chooses to purchase, it may be hard to predict the profits from the book sale. Rather than counting on those dollars immediately, it may be well to designate those profits as seed money for the next author/illustrator visit.

Most of us want to have a successful visit. The motivation is not profit, but to give the children, parents, teachers, and librarians involved a first-hand experience with a talented individual.

Worksheet 8-2: Checklist for Selling Books

SELLING CHECKLIST

Tables and chairs (adequate space to display books and handle purchases)

Books

Calculator

Cash box

For deposit only stamp

Signs

    Book title clearly stating price - including tax

    Checks payable to:_____

    Discount being offered:

    List beneficiary of profits from book sales

Receipts (if needed)

Bags for carrying new purchases

The issue of organizing your audience when it comes to buying books and having books autographed should be addressed. You will need a system of crowd control. Keep the area or lines for selling books separate from the line for getting autographs.

AUTOGRAPHING

Autographing can be handled in several ways. The more usual setting is a long line of people, slightly impatient, but excited about their new acquisition and nervous as the line moves forward. Ideally, each child or family will have time to meet and greet the author or illustrator and be allowed a chance to have a personal conversation. Decide ahead of time if limits will be imposed on how many books can be autographed for each person in line. General guidelines are one or two books per person with the opportunity to go to the end of the line and have additional copies signed if time permits.

Adults can be more obstinate than any group of children when it comes to following the guidelines. Try to be firm but friendly about your decision if it meets with criticism. It is necessary to have guidelines about what books can be autographed. New books, just purchased are the obvious choice. It is probably a good idea not to permit autographing of promotional materials like posters or bookmarks. But will the audience be allowed to bring in books from home, or can the local librarian bring copies from the library's collection to be signed? Have signs that specify what is permitted.

THE AUTOGRAPH TABLE

Make sure that you have enough room for autographing so that your guest and those waiting in line can be comfortable. Provide small papers or post-it notes for people to write names or messages the author or illustrator might need if special requests are allowed, unless these are unneccessary because of already filled out forms. An adult should act as host or hostess to the guest. Be sure the table surface is clean and clear, pens are available, and any special requirements met.

The host's role is to assist by keeping the line moving, helping to get books open to the appropriate page for autographing, acting as a watchdog so the author or illustrator's attention is not monopolized by one person, monitoring and limiting the number of books autographed for any one person.

Lines can be avoided if there is time for your guest to autograph books purchased ahead of time. A note is often inserted in the book with the message the owner wants inscribed. This allows the author/illustrator the luxury of signing books at leisure in a quiet setting. Schools can often organize such an event more easily because each classroom teacher can be responsible for a class. The author can then sign books before or after school.

It is appropriate to have guests sign their books ahead of time and sell the autographed books at the public program. Although the book is not personalized, it is autographed and long lines have been eliminated. This method works if time restraints will not allow either the author or the audience the luxury of a personal interaction.

Another possibility is to have authors sign bookplates that can be attached to the book. This kind of autographing can be done at the author/illustrator's leisure (at home before the visit, on the plane, or even in the hotel room). Bookplates are much easier to carry around than a stack of books! This might be done when the author's book is hot off the press and is being sent directly to the library. When time with the author is limited, plain mailing labels can be autographed and then converted to bookplates. As a book is

Figure 8-2: Author/Illustrator Pat Cummings Autographing Her Books

sold, a bookplate is attached to the frontispiece. One time when attending a library conference, autographed bookplates were distributed by an author to the publisher's guests but the books were later mailed because the publisher knew that we would appreciate not having to weigh down luggage with a thick hardbound book.

Because all youngsters cannot afford to buy a book but would like to have the author's autograph, making an autographed bookmark allows everyone to have the celebrity script in a nice neat format. When an autographed bookmark is not available, kids will begin bringing up any scrap of paper to be signed. Chaos results! This should not be permitted.

Ask your guest to supply you with an autograph in one of your letters of confirmation. Design a bookmark which includes this

Figure 8-3: Author/Poet Arnold Adoff Signs Books for Anxious Fans

special script and a picture or other information on the author or illustrator. Black ink on a white card reproduces well. The experience of getting your guest's autograph needs to be satisfying in the eyes of the child to make the whole event worthwhile.

Worksheet 8-3: Autograph Table Checklist

AUTOGRAPH TABLE CHECKLIST

■ Enough room for your guest to be comfortable

■ Table and chairs

■ Person with people skills to assist author; manage crowds; keep line moving; put people at ease. Tell someone very nicely that what he/she wants is not permitted.

■ Room to open books to pass over to the guest.

■ Paper or post-it notes for writing names and message requests that the author will need to refer to when autographing.

■ Pens and/or pencils.

Figure 8-4: "Cut-out and Make a Bookmark" Autographed by Lee Bennet Hopkins

GOOD BOOKS,
GOOD TIMES!

Good books.

Good times.

Good stories.

Good rhymes.

Good beginnings.

Good ends.

Good people.

Good friends.

Good fiction.

Good facts.

Good adventures.

Good acts.

Good stories.

Good rhymes.

Good books.

Good times.

© 1985 Lee Bennett Hopkins

Art by Marc Brown

Autograph!

Cut on dotted line
and make a bookmark!

Figure 8-5: Drawing From Pat Cummings for Students to Color Before Her Scheduled Visit

Oftentimes, it is the schedule for autographing that is adjusted—or has time stolen from it. Try to avoid disappointing your audience at this point. Accommodate the public in every possible way. Fans are important to the artist. You will need a system of crowd control and organizing your audience when it comes to buying books and having books autographed. Keep the area or lines for selling books separate from the line for getting autographs. Some children may bring books from home, or librarians or teachers may have institution or personal copies of books to be autographed. There is no need for everyone to go through both lines.

9 APPROACHING THE BIG DAY

Make contact with your guest a couple of days before the scheduled visit just to make sure that everything is set. If your guest is already on the road, check-in with a host you know to see how things are going. You can inquire about any last minute changes or adjustments. You are probably familiar with the schedule for the day, so you may want to reaffirm times, names of who will be at the airport, and any other last minute information or instructions that will ensure a positive beginning to your visit. At this time you might want to give your home phone number to your guest as an insurance measure. If problems develop or emergencies arise you will need to be contacted as soon as possible. Your guest's family back home may be happy to know they have your phone number in case of an emergency.

Review and make yourself an edited copy of the itinerary—in detail so you do not forget anything! Reminders to yourself in writing will reassure you. Just don't forget to refer to this schedule. Include directions, addresses, names, phone numbers and the like.

The day will be a big success! Think and act positively. If you are confident, everyone around you will have the same positive expectations and actions. Your careful planning will pay off because everyone will know what they must do, so last minute juggling can be avoided. If your guest is on tour or you have piggybacked with another library or school, and your guest is in your area (or at least you know the location) the day before, call that place and ask how things are going and inquire of any special problems or needs.

You may find out that your guest is coming down with a cold, or that a raincoat was forgotten at the previous day's venture, or that your guest craves chocolate—a nice touch to add to your welcoming basket.

Perhaps you will find out that the formal talk with a large group of children only lasted fifteen minutes and the guest expected the children to ask questions for the remaining time or that the slide show has 100 slides and it takes every minute of an hour program to get through them. Just remind yourself that authors and illustrators are only human, and your only choice is to accept them as they are. However, having just a snippet of information enables you to save the day with minor adjustments.

Preparing some worthwhile questions ahead of time and planting them among the nine- and ten-year-olds in your audience helps ensure that the audience does find out about the talents of your guest. Preparing small signs with the number of minutes left for the

Figure 9-1: Confirmation Letter to Author before His Arrival

Wood County District Public Library ● 251 N. Main St. ● Bowling Green, OH 43402-2477
Telephone: 419/352-5104 ● FAX: 419/354-0405

August 30, 1991

Mr. Lee Bennett Hopkins
Scarborough, NY 10510

Dear Lee:

We're getting ready—full speed ahead!

Here are your flight tickets. Thanks for your cooperation.

Did you say you could send an autogragh to use for a bookmark to hand out to everyone? If you'd send that along, we'd gladly print a supply.

If you can think of any other "complications" or less, don't hesitate to call.

Sincerely,

Kathy East
Head of Children's Services

Walbridge Branch Library	Bradner Branch Library
108 North Main	130 North Main
Walbridge, OH 43465	Bradner, OH 43406
419/666-9900	

Worksheet 9-1: Room Set-Up Checklist

- Comfortable place for guest to wait before the event
- Stage or stage-like setting
- Special decorations or display items made by children
- Chair for guest
- Lectern
- Microphone
- Table with pitcher for water and a glass
- Roped/taped off area
- Chairs/carpet squares
- Books
- Tables for selling books
- Table for autographing books
- Appropriate signs
- Place for book seller
- Cash box and change
- Pens
- Coat rack
- Lighting adjusted
- Assign people to sell books, stack books, assist with autographing, deal with crowd control.
- Check with all locations involved in the visit. Verify any last minute details. Confirm with volunteers, too.

talk may urge a long-winded or slow-moving talk to be wrapped up if the two-minute warning is shown.

Rain, snow, locked doors, flat tires are all possibilities, and can be dealt with as they arise, so get a good night's sleep the night before and move forward.

Figure 9-2: Itinerary for George Ella Lyon

Wood County District Public Library ● 251 N. Main St. ● Bowling Green, OH 43402-2477
Telephone: 419/352-5104 ● FAX: 419/354-0405

October 10, 1990

Ms. Georgia Ella Lyon
Lexington, KY 40504

Dear George Ella:

Thought I'd best touch base with you before I go off to the Ohio Library Association meeting this week.

You have a busy, but wonderful schedule here in Northwest Ohio! Everyone is looking forward to your visit!

The tentative schedule looks like this:

>   Thursday, November 1

>   11:30 A.M. Arrive in Bowling Green (we're straight up I75—almost to Toledo)

>   1-3:15 Conneaut School *one 45 minute session with 4th & 5th graders (in the library)

>   *one 45 minute session with 5th & 6th graders (in the library)

>   *autograph session for these who have purchased books

>   Book and Reader Conference

>   *autographing and Dinner and your talk! (flyer enclosed)

>   Friday, November 2

>   Morning in Perrysburg schools (that's the next burg North)

>   9-1 Frank School second graders

>   10-11 Toth School third graders

>   Lunch-Wood County District Public Library, Bowling Green

Since there's no school on Friday, the library is planning a day of "Homespun Fun." We'll have spinners and quilters and a paper quilt for youngsters to create and we're inviting people to bring a light lunch (in a basket—in honor of <u>Basket</u>) to eat at the library and then to have you share with them that book! There will also be time for autographing . In my mind you will be done by 2 P.M. (although our activities may extend a bit longer!)

Of course, we'll have people to squire you around and a motel reservation and food and honorarium—but I suggest you rest up and come strong and brave!

I hope you're still planning to head North on Wednesday evening. That should get you to Bowling Green in good time.

My only request is that you send me your autograph on the enclosed sheet of paper and I'll make a gift bookmark for the classes you visit!

Call me if you have question, although I'll send even more details next week.

Happy Halloween planning!

Fondly,

Kathy East

Walbridge Branch Library	Bradner Branch Library
108 North Main	130 North Main
Walbridge, OH 43465	Bradner, OH 43406
419/666-9900	

Figure 9-3: Itinerary for Pat Cummings

ITTINERARY FOR PAT CUMMINGS

(from Kathy East
Coordinato of Children's and Young Adult Services,
Public Library of Columbys and Franklin County
Work 614-864-8000050
Home 614-888-9923

Wednesday, February 20

10:30 A.M.	Arrival—are we pleased!
	Getting to know Columbus, the Public Library of Columbus and Franklin County and getting settled at the Christopher Inn, 300 East Broad, 614-228-3541
	LUNCH
2.00 P.M.	"Chalk Talk"
	Driving Park Branch Library
	1566 East Livingston Avenue
	614-222-395
	Gloria Campbell, Branch Manager
	Classes from:
	The Jewish Center
	Sunshine Christian School
	Southeast Christian School
	One Head Start Program
4-5 P.M.	Autogaph Session
	Cover-to-Cover Bookstore
	3337 North High Street
	614-253-1624
	Sally Oddi, Owner
5:30 P.M.	Supper at Marble Gang Restaurant
	1062 Mt. Vernon Avenue, 614-253-7696
	with Gloria Campbell, Shirley Walker, Rubye Kyles, you and me!
7:30 P.M.	Bedtime "Chalk Talk" Story Time
	Martin Luther King Branch
	1600 East Long Street
	614-222-7122
	Autograph session and snacks
	Return to Christopher Inn (don't forget to contact Virginaa Hamilton)

Thursday, February 21

8:30 A.M.	Pick up by Shirley Walker
9:00 A.M.	"How to ....." with art students
	Martin Luther King Branch
	Junior high kids from Franklin Middle School and East High School
10:30 A.M.	Pick up from visit
	519 Trevitt Elementary School
	614-252-4963
	Nancy Zook, Teacher
	"Chalk Talk" with 40 kids or so (2-3 representatives from each of their 4th and 5th frade classes)
Noon	Leave for airport and lunch
2:01 P.M.	Departure from Port Coumbus and collapse!

HOSTING A RECEPTION

You may want to schedule a reception after the presentation and autograph session to give people an opportunity to meet and mingle with the author or illustrator.

There is something about having treats or the traditional punch and cookies after an event which adds to the celebration. A reception creates an informal setting for people to talk and get to know one another better. It gives the people a reason to linger after a program. For many youngsters a reception held to honor an author or an illustrator may be their introduction to the social graces involved.

RECEPTION COSTS

The cost of providing refreshments, the time available for a reception, the amount of room and the number of people expected needs to be taken into account when considering a reception.

Refreshments mean hospitality. You and your committee will need to decide how much work you want your reception to entail.

Worksheet 9-2: Reception Checklist

Reception Checklist

- Room booked
- Budget set and food decided
- Caterer contacted/donations lined up
- Room arrangement planned
- Table arrangement planned
- Supplies ordered/gathered
- Tablecloth
- Centerpiece
- Coffee pots/punch bowls
- Cups
- Napkins
- Trays/platters
- Wastebaskets

Many choices of food and drink makes the line passing the refreshment table move slowly. Try serving from both sides of the table. If you are expecting a large crowd or are unsure of how many people might attend the reception and consume refreshments, choose a simple menu—for example, finger foods or cupcakes.

Finger Foods

Finger foods—for example, little sandwiches, cookies, brownies, nuts, and the traditional sweet platter means that fewer utensils are needed. You don't need to put out all of the cookies or nuts at one time. Extra cookies can easily be frozen and nuts can be put in airtight containers and stored for the next celebration.

Cupcakes

Cupcakes are neat and the clean-up is a breeze. They can be decorated in a multitude of ways—to coincide with characters from the author's or illustrator's stories, school colors, etc. (Sheet cakes are a common choice, too.)

Fruit

In keeping with healthier eating habits, fruit may be a good choice for your reception. A watermelon boat filled with fruit pieces can be served as the main dish in a fancier buffet. In an informal setting consider a basketful of apples or some other hand-held fruits.

Beverages

Having only punch to drink simplifies planing as well. A simple punch with few ingredients—fruit juice and 7-Up with a fruit filled ice ring is attractive—and makes mixing the punch convenient. Additional ingredients can be opened and added as needed.

When many adults will be part of the audience coffee should be served—whether it is a daytime or evening reception, always include decaffeinated coffee as well as regular. Also make sure you have a pot of hot water for tea and hot chocolate. Don't forget to include spoons, stirrers, sugar, tea bags, and hot chocolate packets.

Theme Receptions

If the author or illustrator's books are about a circus, a fair, or have a baseball theme, why not serve popcorn, roasted peanuts, or cotton candy? You can also use a birthday cake, raw vegetables, or even

Worksheet 9-3: Refreshments Idea List

REFRESHMENTS IDEA LIST

Be creative! Consider serving:

- Punch and Cookies
- Apples and Popcorn
- Root Beer Floats
- Mini Muffins
- Cupcakes
- Fruit Cup
- Banana Splits
- Make Your Own Sundaes
- Cider and Doughnuts
- Ants On A Log (raisins on top of peanut butter filled celery slices)
- Peanuts, Raisins, and Dried Fruit (trail mix)
- Tea and Chocolate
- Mini Bagels and Cream Cheese
- Ice Cream Cones or Ice Cream in a Cup
- Inspired???

soup to reinforce to the audience the titles or topics of illustrations or stories shared.

DECORATIONS

Decorations make a dull area come alive! You may be able to choose a theme for your reception which carries out an idea or reinforces something from your guest's books. For example, a circus theme, an "under the sea" theme, a rodeo theme, etc.

PHOTOGRAPHS

Plan to capture the thrill of this special event by taking pictures for your library or school scrapbook. Have children in the photographs. Capture their excitement and awe as they watch and listen. Snap a picture of your guest equally enthralled with the audience's attention.

Figure 9-4: Room Decorated with Baskets for George Ella Lyon's Visit Based on Her Book *Baskets*

Mention to your guest that you would like to record their visit and some of the activities with photographs. If your guest has a problem having photographs taken and wants to restrict them, you must know that early on and convey that information to your audience.

Discuss arrangements to allow individual children or classes to have photos taken with the guest. Some parents or children may bring a camera from home and will want to have a personal photo taken sometime during the program. Decide with your guest when he or she thinks the most appropriate time will be—most likely during autographing.

Make a member of your planning committee responsible for taking all the photographs or for recruiting a volunteer photographer. Don't forget to keep in mind the expense of film and the cost of developing the pictures and having copies made.

Successful photographs make for fond memories. Include the photos in the thank you note to serve as a tangible remembrance for your guest too.

Figure 9-5: Photograph of Poet/Anthologist Lee Bennet Hopkins During His Presentation

PRESS/MEDIA EVENT

When you plan a media event have extra copies of the publisher's promotional materials about your guest available for all the media outlets. You may want to hold a special event and invite the local newspaper reporters and television cameras for some authors or illustrators.

The rededication of a children's area (after expansion or remodeling) could be such a happening. Although the building may look the same on the outside, a whole new atmosphere may now exist in the children's department. The cutting of a ribbon, the first use of the new storytelling area, or the unveiling of an original piece of art done by your guest all qualify as news. Although the media are there, some may choose to have a more in-depth interview with your guest.

THE BIG DAY

This is the big day you have been planning and waiting for such a long time it hardly seems possible that this is it! As coordinator of the event you probably have that deep sense of responsibility and will have planned your day to revolve around most of your guest's activities.

Homey Touches

Don't forget the nice touches. A vase of fresh flowers on the autograph table adds to the attractiveness of the setting. Having a corsage or boutonniere for your guest to wear is a special gift and helps to identify the guest for your audience. A special name tag may be an appropriate welcoming gift. A small basket of fruit or a bag of area products or snacks is a tasty treat.

Visit Memorabilia

Items with information about your library on them—bookbag, coffee mug, or bookmark—all serve as a nice remembrance of where this visit was staged for your guest.

A fond memory for a guest, is the artwork, notes, or messages from the children. If something special is created, like a scrapbook, a photo album, or an original book of some sort, this gift should be presented to your guest. Sheer size may mean the gift needs to be mailed back to your guest's home, so be ready to make that offer.

Private Time

Allow private time for the author to do some local shopping or browsing and/or resting up. The day will be tiring, so try not to overdo the number of activities for yourself or the guest. Set a pace that is realistic. Avoid rushing from one place to another.

Remember that your guest may have special requests or needs of which you are unaware until he or she arrives. Be sensitive to the guest's needs, particularly medical needs, like the importance of eat-

---

Worksheet 9-4: Big Day Checklist

BIGDAY CHECKLIST

- The day's schedule
- Flowers or welcoming gift
- Special name tags
- A city map and/or directions
- Introduction
- Invoice
- Check
- Any other paperwork
- Cash in case some supply or need must be met on short notice

---

ing at specific times for a diabetic. Occasionally dietary needs can cause an embarrassment if last minute adjustments are not made.

If one person is escorting the guest all day long it becomes easier to anticipate needs. The level of comfort will grow with this stranger, so requests may become easier to make, but be aware and do not let a guest go all day without a coffee break or a few minutes to sit alone in a comfortable chair. If your guest smokes, you need to be prepared and know how to provide time and a place for that activity. Often a copy of a daily paper, or information about your area from the local Chamber of Commerce makes for interesting and appreciated reading.

You and Your Guest

It is often nice for you, if you are acting as host, to schedule some time with your guest. If you need to pick him/her up at the airport, the ride back may provide the time for some sharing. You have worked hard putting all of this together, so you deserve some small perk, and this may be it! This time together may offer you insight into what to expect or what is expected.

You may gain information to help personalize your introduction or you may realize that a microphone will definitely be needed if a whole auditorium full of people will be able to hear every word.

WHAT'S IN AN INTRODUCTION?

This is a special guest and a special introduction is in order. The best introductions for authors and illustrators come from being familiar with their works. Before the visit it is imperative that you read and study the books written and/or illustrated by your guest. Again, the publisher may promise a media package with educational background and formal training information that will be of interest to your audience. You must take into account your audience or audiences: two or three different introductions may be needed if your guest speaks to preschoolers in the morning, a class of junior high art students in the afternoon and a group of teachers after school.

Acknowledgments and recognitions are often a necessary part of an introduction. Thanks to the funding group or groups is also a requirement.

Consider including something about the audience for the speaker if the connection is not obvious. For example, you might say,

> *"Children have come from all over Franklin County and have checked out your books to read about Bunnicula before you arrived. Some may not even know how to say this famous rabbit's name. Could you start by telling us more."*

SPECIAL TOPICS

Perhaps you have requested a special topic for this talk to librarians and teachers. Or you may know this guest supports a specific issue or cause and may want to mention it in their remarks. Suggestions like *"How do you suggest using poetry regularly in the classroom?"* or *"How have censorship controversies influenced your own choice of topics or vocabulary for your books?"* may be good discussion starters. Your comments may stimulate questions from the audience at the end of the program. Your introduction does not need to be lengthy. Be sincere and welcoming. Then enjoy the talk or presentation.

Figure 9-6: Sample Introduction

INTRODUCTION FOR PAT CUMMINGS

"How many of you scribbled a drawing or doodle during one of the mini sessions you attended? Have you been drawing ever since you can remember?"

That's what Pat Cummings says when asked, When did you become an illustrator?

You might feel as I do, that the difference between what I draw and what Pat does is TALENT! Small word, but big meaning.

"We are pleased to get to know this talented artist and writer and obviously share her labors of love.

Fred's First Day by Cathy Warren and illustrated by Pat is a special book to me because in 1985 or so when I first met Pat, I was fascinated with her explanation of the design of this book about starting school and the confusion in mind and actions on the first day of school and how eventually things begin to organize themselves . . . just as the crayons and the blocks in this picture book!

I also think this book's creation got Pat thinking about writing her own words to illustrate rather than be limited to some other author's words.

And what success! Of course, having family experiences to rely upon—wonderful creations are born—who can deny the fun of Clean Your Room, Harvey Moon!

Pat Cummings is a graduate of the Pratt Institute, lives in Brooklyn with a New York City view that could prove inspirational.

She's a world traveler . . . from childhood as an Army brat to just last week. She has just returned from an African trip to Ghana!

Pat may I present to you the cream of the crop of Ohio educators—in the broadest of definitions—anxious to get to know you better and to lead children to your books and the joy of reading and writing and drawing!

Let us welcome Pat Cummings -"

10 EVALUATING THE EVENTS

Surviving the whole event is the first sign of success! And a quiet sense of satisfaction is a good clue, too. In fact a day or two after the event is a perfect time to have an evaluation meeting. At the last planning meeting, schedule when the evaluation meeting will be, as a natural follow-up.

Reactions and emotions are still fresh in your mind right after the visit. Time has not allowed details to escape. The guest and his/her enthusiasm and skill accounts for the greatest feeling of success. Audience satisfaction also plays a big part in evaluating the program.

Review attendance numbers. Evaluate in response to publicity. What impact did the availability of books for autographing have on the overall event?

With some groups you may choose to use an evaluation form. Allow some open-ended questions on the evaluation form—for example, *"What would you like to see done differently with our next author visit?"* If you used an evaluation form with audiences or asked each of the planning committee members to complete an evaluation, these forms can be reviewed at the meeting.

A question that generates a variety of answers is *"What author/illustrator would you like to have visit in the future?"* The requests may not be realistic, but the statement does give you a sense of names the community knows and values.

Many times the responses on evaluation forms are predictable, but there are always some attendees who will really capture something that you missed. Or something will be said which influences future planning. Do not be surprised when you hear about how hard the chairs were or are asked why the air conditioning could not be controlled. Creature comforts are frequently the most popular topic. Sometimes the smallest details get the longest discussion at the evaluation meeting. That may not be all bad.

The procurement of funds is always a topic for evaluation. It is possible to get the same or additional funding another time? How does that influence your future planning?

As part of the meeting make assignments for the remaining chores to finalize the visit.

- Sending back books
- Writing thank yous
- Reconciling all accounts

Figure 10-1: Thank You Note to Author of *Bunnicula*, James Howe

PUBLIC LIBRARY of COLUMBUS and FRANKLIN COUNTY
28 SOUTH HAMILTON RD.
COLUMBUS, OHIO 43213

October 23, 1985

Mr. James Howe

Wow! James Howe!

Your bookmark spoke true! Thanks for much so visiting the Public Library of Columbus and Franklin County and being the first author to visit the Whetstone branch. Needless to say they were pleased to have you as their guest.

The kids sure do like your books—but you <u>must</u> think of a good story for the origin of Bunnicula! Your patience with the kids was admirable. Keep up the <u>great</u> work.

One side story—the Monday evening after your visit, I was frosting some cupcakes and wanted to tint the frosting pink and blue. I went to the cupboard and took out the little package of food coloring. Everyone of the little bottles was full but the liquid was <u>clear</u>. My exclamation was, "Bunnicula's been here!" I wonder if the Worthington Inn has anything to report after your visit?

Take care. Happy writing—and happily remember Brad and Jason's giggling!

Fondly,

Kathy East
Coordinator of Children's and Young Adult Services

P. S. I shouldn't pick on Brad. Last Sunday he walked 10 miles as part of the CROP Hunger Walk—a real physical feat. He even commented on walking by "the library where I saw Mr. Howe." 'Spose it'll always be your library! (Be writing books to fill it up!)

Take time to outline the thank you letter to your guest and to the publisher. If you can offer constructive criticism, do send your comments to the publisher.

WAS IT WORTH IT?

The toughest answer may be to the question, *"Was it worth it?"* One can happily say, most groups say, yes, and proceed to smooth out and streamline their procedures.

If the answer to the question is no, try to analyze the responses. Obviously author/illustrator visits can be very successful and are repeated regularly in schools, libraries, and at conferences.

The ultimate satisfaction should be that this event and all the planning and work that went into it was a learning experience for all, children and adults alike.

Figure 10-2: Thank You Memo to Staff for a Successful Author Visit

MEMO

DATE: October 24, 1985

TO: Marilyn and the Whetstone Staff

FROM: Kathy East

RE: James Howe Visit

This is a big "thanks" for making James Howe's visit to Whetstone such a successful event.

Everyone was very friendly and cooperative. I think that shows a real "team" spirit on your part.

I know Mr. Howe was very relaxed and truly enjoyed his presentations. Don't kids ask the craziest questions?

"Thank you" to each of you for your own contribution. May visits by all of your special guests in the future go as smoothly!

KAE/

11 ALTERNATIVES

There are some alternatives to having an author or illustrator actually be *in* your library for a visit. Perhaps you live in a remote area and the sheer distances involved make a real live visit unlikely.

A TELECONFERENCE

In this method, phone lines make a person-to-person visit possible. A conference call is scheduled through a telephone operator. The planning stages involve setting a date and time for a visit and interview or at least some form of two-way conversation.

This mini-visit is very successful (and impressive) if a small group or a single classroom has a real interest in a specific individual because of their expertise or style. Have the guest prepare some opening remarks or a short address, but the true test comes when children and students begin asking specific questions.

A picture of the group to be talked with should be given to the author or illustrator ahead of time so a real sense of knowing one another develops.

A classroom can send a picture clearly labeled so when a question is asked, the author can quickly find the right face to go with the voice. With a spontaneously gathered group the picture may need to be a follow-up gift!

Questions should be prepared ahead of time, to avoid wasting precious time and to help develop a logical sequence to the questions and assure some learning objectives are met.

The teleconference is appealing to authors and illustrators because it enables them to remain in their own work setting. Their work time may be interrupted, but the amount is much less than if they had to leave their home and travel halfway across the country.

Artists often welcome such interruptions because they are enriched and rewarded by the interest, enthusiasm, and honesty of their audiences. Many writers say they write from their own experience but none deny the boost and sense of satisfaction gained when they meet with young audiences.

The success of this style of visit may prove so pleasant and cost effective that it may be easy to replicate it several times a year.

EDUCATIONAL TELEVISION/CABLE HOOK-UP

This method of visiting with an author or illustrator is one often sponsored or carried out by state libraries, state departments of education, or educational television franchises. Authors and

---

Worksheet 11-1: Teleconference Planning Checklist

- Contact a publisher to explore and to coordinate a phone visit with a particular artist

- Inquire about honorarium

- Get permission for a teleconference from the administration

- Explore the availability of phone lines and equipment (speaker, phone, etc.)

- Reserve, rent, arrange for equipment needed

- Do homework on cost per minute of such a phone hook-up (taking into account long distance rates and the planned length of the call)

- Plan a fund raising event or drive to underwrite the cost of the teleconference

- Set goals and specific activities to precede, accompany, and follow-up the actual phone call

- Evaluate the impact on children's choices in reading

- Monitor verbal reaction to the teleconference

---

illustrators are invited to a television studio to promote their work. Sometimes a group of children is invited as well.

The presence of an audience often makes the visit easier for the author or illustrator. The attention, nods of heads, even questionable looks of the audience help the speaker to know if what is being said is being understood.

Any number of classrooms or other educational settings can receive the broadcast of the author's presentation. When an illustrator is the guest, the television camera affords such a close up view of the action, the viewer feels it is almost better than being a member of the live audience. With the addition of a telephone hook-up, youngsters from any of the sites can call in their questions and comments.

Authors and illustrators seem pleased with the cable television format. Such a visit certainly is a convenient way to reach many youngsters in a single presentation.

VIDEO VISITS

The success of author and illustrator visits has greatly increased the demand for visits. Publishers can well be proud!

Considering the growing expense involved in inviting an author or illustrator, and the possible time artists could be away from their workplaces, some publishing houses have begun producing video visits. High quality productions offer the feeling of a personal visit.

Oftentimes, the video follows the production of a single manuscript from start to finish. Because many youngsters are curious about how a book is made, this demonstration tape can answer many questions. A visit to the author's home or studio as well as the opportunity to meet his/her family is often featured in the video.

The demonstrations of art techniques are certainly clearly shown and they are a lot less messy on video. Occasionally research sites are favorite places for inspiration and are shown to audiences through the video.

These 30 to 60 minute visits with authors and illustrators can be used as an introduction to a person and personal style. This seemingly first-hand visit can encourage interest in an author's writings, bring meaning to an illustrator's techniques or introduce a youngster to the care and passion put into the research process when writing a book. Hearing the author's or illustrator's voice has the magical power of turning youngsters to their books.

However, please note that it is not ethical to use a video tape that was not provided by a publishing company without the prior consent of the author. Some authors are justifiably concerned that a successful appearance might have been recorded without their knowledge and distributed to numerous schools, making an actual visit from them unnecessary. Also, for this reason, do not be surprised if you have a visiting author who requests that no video or audiotaping be permitted during their talk.

SUMMARY

All three alternative visits require many of the same planning steps described for a real-life visit by an author or illustrator. Review the planning checklist and get going!

Whatever the format, a sincere effort to bring children to the realization and appreciation of the work of authors and illustrators by introducing them to these people has proved to be a satisfying experience. When this meeting inspires youngsters to read and encourages an appreciation for books, all the planning and effort are worthwhile.

12 HANDLING AWKWARD MOMENTS

THINGS THAT HAVE HAPPENED WITH SOME GUESTS

How would you like to see these incidents handled? They are given to alert you to unforeseen occurrences that can and do arise. We have not supplied answers because each solution must be geared to its own situation.

1. When working with three other groups to plan and carry out an author or illustrator's visit, one of the committee members is being very petty, only wanting to pay mileage for the exact number of miles from your library to their community center, and only for the lunch before the presentation at their center and only for the exact number of bookmarks given to the audience at their programs.

2. When checking with your guest two weeks before the visit, you find out he or she is recovering from surgery. What adjustments would you be willing to make?

3. On short notice you find out a planned three-day visit needs to be changed to only one day or canceled completely.

4. Your guest makes all of the travel arrangements and arrives a day early.

5. Your guest arrives with a whole entourage of people. This can happen as part of a publisher's tour. What do you do with the extra people? Even more complicated is the time when your guest arrives with the whole family and everyone expects to be treated as your guests.

6. Because of a plane delay, you consolidated two morning presentations into one at one of the elementary schools. Now the PTO only wants to pay half of the originally agreed upon honorarium.

7. Your guest has been on a publisher's tour for several weeks doing two or three autographing sessions a day. When you meet at the airport your guest is quite ill—tired, feverish, exhausted.

8. Your guest's spouse makes six long distance calls, collect to you, just checking in, during a two-day visit at your library.

9. Your guest wakes up with laryngitis.

10. You have made arrangements for a rather formal dinner party honoring your guest. Your guest arrives in jeans and tennis shoes.

11. Your guest has a medical emergency. How would you handle a trip to the emergency room of the hospital?

12. When you stand near your guest, you are sure you can smell alcohol.

13. It's your first author visit and you've made all the arrangements. You ordered books and now you realize you have no outside group (there is no Friends or PTO group) to work with you. How can you sell the books at cost and yet assure there will be dollars to cover the shipping costs and the cost to return any unsold copies?

14. Your guest is approached by someone from the audience who has brought his or her own original manuscript and asks the guest to critique the work. Or the author is asked to take the work with them and send it back with comments. Or your guest is asked for a recommendation of what publisher might accept a manuscript or portfolio of drawings.

15. You are shocked when your guest makes sexual advances toward you when you are alone.

16. You are part of a week long series of visits among several schools. On Tuesday the snow starts falling; Wednesday is your day to host the author or illustrator. The grapevine talk says Wednesday will be a snow day! (Or imagine some other weather/power emergency).

17. Two weeks after the author visit, two boxes of new books arrive from the publisher.

APPENDIX A

AUTHOR VISIT PLANNING CHECKLIST/WORKSHEET

It may say author visit, but these guidelines apply for any others whom you may have as guests: a ventriloquist, puppeteers, book reviewers, book/magazine editors, publishers, and workshop speakers and leaders.

Use them for any visit where transportation, housing, honoraria, equipment, and publicity are part of the planning process. Using the elements of this planning checklist will help lead to a successful visit.

Brainstorm (Dream) early!

Build from a pool of authors and illustrators you have heard/seen/met.

List your preferences:

1.

2.

3.

4.

5.

Talk to someone who has heard/seen/knows the author or illustrator.

- Peers or co-workers who attend state, regional, and national conferences

- Librarians or teachers in your area

- A publicist you know and whose judgment you trust

Do some homework on your preferred list of people.

- Know their books; check, update your collection

- Where do they live?

- Have you seen information on their visits to other schools, libraries?

Work through the publisher.

- Contact the publisher
- Propose dates (be flexible)
- Ask about kinds of presentations; propose *your* program
- Inquire about honoraria
- Inquire about other costs (travel, housing, etc.)

Be realistic about the money you can spend for an honorarium plus expenses.

- Define and agree on an honorarium. Agree on who will make travel and lodging arrangements. Know who will pay the bills for meals, travel, and hotel room.

Build coalitions. Share planning, publicity, expenses, etc.

Ask:	Contact Person:
Schools	_____
Other libraries	_____
Bookstores	_____
Child advocacy groups	_____
Community groups	_____
Businesses	_____

Confirm event with guest, publisher, planning committee, sites involved.

Keep confidential information shared (home address, phone number, social security number, etc.).

Be very specific about what you plan and what you expect to have happen.

Cover:

- Program format
- Day, date, time

- Location
- Autographing circumstances
- Travel arrangements
- Housing arrangements
- Honorarium
- Billing/paying procedure
- Host/hostesses names

Develop detailed itinerary.

- Follow- up telephone conversations with a letter - every *time!*
- Dates

Request publicity materials from publicist.

- Background information
- Photograph
- About the author flyer
- Free bookmarks
- Free posters
- Galleys of most current work

Arrange for local publicity.

- Printing needs (posters, flyers, bookmarks)
- Local paper, television station, radio station (press releases and interviews)

Order books/materials for selling/autographing.

- *Order/procedure*
- Minimum order requirements
- Discount offer
- Return policy
- Billing/payment arrangements (usually through Friends of the Library or PTO)

Have telephone follow-up two weeks or so before visit.

- Confirm arrival time
- Confirm meeting time/place
- Confirm name of host/hostess
- Give final directions
- Ask if any changes or needs in supplies or equipment

Confirm local arrangements.

- Reservations
- Hosts
- Room arrangement
- Equipment needs
- Autographing details (books, cash box etc.)
- Itinerary
- Check and/or business forms

Enjoy the visit!

- Welcome your guest with flowers or a basket of fruit in their room
- Show off your city, libraries, or schools
- Allow guest time to rest

- Allow guest time to be alone
- Treat them as someone special, *they are!*

Have business talk with guest upon arrival.

- Request invoice
- Request receipts
- Check/verify other paperwork

Write thank you notes!

- To the guest
- To the publicist (be honest here)
- To any special group or person who made *your* job easier
- To those who *funded* the visit

APPENDIX B

LISTING OF CHILDREN'S BOOK PUBLISHERS AND THEIR CONTACTS

Artists And Writers Guild Books
See Western Publishing Co., Inc.

Atheneum Books For Children
See Simon & Schuster Children's Publishing

Avon Books
1350 Avenue of the Americas
New York, NY 10019
212-261-6800
Gwen Montgomery, Editorial Director, Books
    for Young Readers
Dorothy Millhofer, Contact

Bantam Doubleday Dell Books for Young Readers
1540 Broadway
New York, NY 10036
212-354-6500
Terry Barzumoto, Contact
Craig Virden, Vice-President and Publisher

Beech Tree Books
1350 Avenue of the Americas
New York, NY 10019
212-261-6500
Paulette Clark Kaufmann, Editor-in-Chief and
    Vice-President William Morrow & Co., Inc.
Lori Benton, Contact

Bradbury Press
See Simon & Schuster Children's Publishing

Bridgewater Books
(An imprint of Troll Associates)
100 Corporate Drive
Mahwah, NJ. 07430
201-529-4000

Bonnie Brook, Associate Publisher
Linda Lannon, Director of Sales and Marketing

Browndeer Press
See Harcourt Brace and Company

Carolrhoda Books, Inc.
241 First Avenue North
Minneapolis, MN 55401
612-332-3344
Emily Kelley, Editorial Director
Jeff Reynolds, Director of Marketing, Lerner
    Group

Charlesbridge Publishing
85 Main Street
Watertown, MA 02172
617-926-0329
Mary Ann Sabia, General Manager, Trade
    Division
Brent Farmer, President

Children's Book Press
6400 Hollis Street, Suite 4
Emeryville, CA 94608
510-655-3395
Harriet Rohmer, Publisher
Emily Romero, Marketing Assistant

Children's Press
See Grolier, Inc.

Chronicle Books
275 Fifth Street
San Francisco, CA 94103
415-777-7240
Melissa Hosmer, Contact

Clarion Books
See Houghton Mifflin Inc.

Cobblehill Books
See Penguin USA

Crown Publishers
See Random House, Inc.

Dial Books for Young Readers
See Penguin USA

Disney Book Publishing, Inc
114 Fifth Avenue
New York, NY 10011
212-633-4400
Lauren L. Wohl, Marketing Director, Disney
    Juvenile Publishing
Tom Quash, Contact
Children's imprints include Disney Press,
    Hyperion Books for Children

Dorling Kindersley Inc.
95 Madison Avenue
New York, NY 10016
212-213-4800
Dagmar Greve, Director of Library Marketing
Alan Benjamin, Editor

Dutton Children's Books
See Penguin USA

Enslow Publishers, Inc.
44 Fadem Road
Box 699
Springfield, NJ 07081-0699
201-379-8890
Mark Enslow, President
Brian D. Enslow, Vice-President Editorial

Farrar, Straus, & Giroux, Inc.
19 Union Square West
New York, NY 10003
212-741-6900
Michael Eisenberg, Vice-President, Associate
    Publisher, and Marketing Director Books for
    Young Readers
Debbie Hochman, Contact

Four Winds Press
See Simon & Schuster Children's Publishing

Golden Books
See Western Publishing Co.

Greenwillow Books
See William Morrow & Co.

Grolier, Inc.
Sherman Turnpike
Danbury, CT 06816
203-797-3500
Amy Kaufman, Contact
Children's imprints include Children's Press,
    Franklin Watts

Grosset & Dunlap, Inc.
See Putnam and Grosset Group

Gulliver Books
See Harcourt Brace and Company

Harcourt Brace and Company
525 B Street
Suite 1900
San Diego, CA 92101
619-699-6810
Louis Howton, Vice-President, Director HP
    Trade Division Children's Books
Jane Washburn, Contact

Children's imprints include Browndeer Press, Gulliver Books

Harper Trophy Paperbacks
See HarperCollins Children's Books

HarperCollins Children's Books
10 East 53rd Street
New York, NY 10022
212-207-7044
Lisa Holton, Vice-President, Associate Publisher, and Editor-in-Chief
Catherine Balkin, Contact
Children's imprints include Harper Trophy Paperbacks

Holiday House
425 Madison Avenue
New York, NY 10017
212-688-0085
Kate H. Briggs, Vice-President and Director of Marketing
Dianne Foote, Contact

Henry Holt and Company, Inc.
115 West 18th Street
New York, NY 10011
212-886-9200
Brenda Bowen, Associate Publisher and Vice-President Books for Young Readers
Beth Feldman, Marketing Director, Books for Young Readers

Houghton Mifflin Inc.
222 Berkeley Street
Boston, MA 02116
617-351-5000
Walter H. Lorraine, Director, Children's Books
Jennifer Roberts, Marketing Manager, Children's Books
Children's imprints include Clarion Books

Hyperion Books for Children
See Disney Books for Children

Jewish Lights Publishing
P.O. Box 237
Route 4
Sunset Farm Offices
Woodstock, VT 05091
802-457-4000
Sandra Korinchak, Marketing Manager
Stuart M. Matlins, President/Publisher

Kingfisher Books
95 Madison Avenue
New York, NY 10016
212-481-9403
Wendy Barish, Associate Publisher
Beth Eller, Director of Marketing

Alfred A. Knopf, Inc.
See Random House, Inc.

Lee & Low Books
95 Madison Avenue
New York, NY 10017
212-779-4400
Philip Lee, Publisher
Elizabeth Szabla, Editor-in-Chief

Lerner Publications Company
241 First Avenue North
Minneapolis, MN 55401
612-332-3344
Nancy M. Campbell, Editorial Director
Mary Winget, Editor

Little, Brown, & Co.
34 Beacon Street
Boston, MA 02108
617-227-0730

Maria Modgno, Vice-President and Editor-in-Chief, Children's Books
Kathy Rourke, Contact

Lothrop, Lee & Shepard Books
See William Morrow & Co.

Macmillan Books for Young Readers
See Simon and Schuster Children's Publishing

Margaret K. McElderry Books
See Simon and Schuster Children's Publishing

The Millbrook Press, Inc.
2 Old New Milford Road
Brookfield, CT 06804
203-740-2220
Jean E. Reynolds, President
Elaine Pascoe, Editor-in-Chief

William Morrow & Company
1350 Avenue of the Americas
New York, NY 10019
212-261-6500
Susan Hirschman, Editor-in-Chief and Senior Vice-President
Jazan Higgins, Vice-President and Director of Children's Book Marketing
Children's imprints include Greenwillow Books, Morrow Junior Books, Mulbery Books, Tambourine Books

Morrow Junior Books
See William Morrow & Co.

Mulberry Books
See William Morrow & Co.

NBM Publishing
185 Madison Avenue, Suite 1504
New York, NY 10016
212-545-1223
Terry Nantier, President

North-South Books
1123 Broadway
Suite 800
New York, NY 10010
212-463-9736
Marc Cheshire, Vice-President and Publisher
Kathleen Fogarty, Vice-President, Director of Sales and Marketing

Orchard Books
95 Madison Avenue
New York, NY 10016
212-686-7070
Neal Porter, President and Publisher

Peachtree Publishers, Ltd.
494 Armour Circle, NE
Atlanta, GA 30324-4088
404-876-8761
Kathy Landwehr, Marketing and Publicity Manager

Peel Productions
P.O. Box 185
Molalla, OR 97038-0185
503-829-6849
Susan DuBosque, Editorial Director
Doug DuBosque, Marketing Director

Pelican Publishing Company, Inc.
P.O. Box 3110
Gretna, LA 70054
504-368-1175
Kathleen Calhoun, Promotion Director
Jan Fehrman, Western Marketing Manager

Penguin USA
375 Hudson Street
New York, NY 10014
212-366-2000
Elena Rockman, Contract
Children's imprints include Cobblehill Books,
    Dutton Childrens Books, Lodestar Books,
    Puffin Books, Viking, Frederick Warne & Co.

Philomel Books
See Putnam & Grosset Group

Pleasant Company
8400 Fairway Place
P.O. Box 991
Middleton, WI 53562
800-233-0264
Janice Blankenburg, Publisher
Lois Jacos, Marketing and Sales Manager

Pocket Books
See Simon & Schuster Children's Publishing

Portunus Publishing Co.
3435 Ocean Park Blvd.
Suite 203
Santa Monica, CA 90405
310-452-2601
Richard A. Schneider, Owner/President
Mirta Pejuan, Office Manager

Puffin Books
See Penguin USA

G.P. Putnam's, Sons
See Putnam & Grosset Group

Putnam & Grosset Group
200 Madison Avenue
New York, NY 10016
212-951-8700

Margaret Frith, President, The Putnam &
    Grosset Group
Greg Galloway, Contact
Children's imprints include Grosset & Dunlap,
    Philomel Books, G.P. Putnam's, Sons

Random House, Inc.
201 East 50th Street
New York, NY 10022
212-751-2600
Janet Schulman, Publisher and Division Vice-
    President Books for Young Readers
Kerry Ryan, Publicity Associate, Books for
    Young Readers
Children's imprints include Crown books for
    Young Readers, Knopf Books for Young
    Readers

Rizzoli International Publications Inc.
300 Park Avenue South
New York, NY 10010
212-387-3400
Manuela Soares, Senior Editor, Children's Books
Amelia Durand, Senior Publicist

RVS Books Inc.
P.O. Box 683
Lebanon, TN 37087
615-449-6725
Bettye W. Shelton, Corporate Secretary and
    Treasurer

Scholastic Hardcover
555 Broadway
New York, NY 10012-3999
212-343-6100
Jean Feiwel, Editor-in-Chief and Division Vice-
    President
John Mason, Marketing Manager, Trade Books

Scholastic Inc.
555 Broadway
New York, NY 10012-3999
212-343-6100
Jean Feiwel, Editor-in-Chief and Division Vice-President
Jacquelyn Harper, Contact

Scientific American Books for Young Readers
(An imprint of W.H. Freeman)
41 Madison Avenue, 37th Floor
New York, NY 10010
212 576-9450
Marc Gave, Executive Editor
Sloane W. Lederer, Trade Sales and Marketing Director

Charles Scribner's Sons
See Simon & Schuster Children's Publishing

Sierra Club Books
100 Bush Street, 13th Floor
San Francisco, CA 94104
415-291-1619
Helen Sweetland, Editor-in-Chief Children's Books

Simon & Schuster Books For Young Readers
See Simon & Schuster Children's Publishing

Simon & Schuster Children's Publishing
866 Third Avenue
New York, NY 10022
212-702-2000
Carol Roeder, Associate Publisher and Vice-President, Sales and Marketing
Elena Blanco, Contact
Children's imprints include Atheneum Books for Children, Bradbury Press, Four Winds Press, Macmillan Books for Young Readers, Simon & Schuster Books for Young Readers

Starseed Press
(An imprint of H.J. Kramer, Inc.)
P.O. Box 1082
Tiburon, CA 94920
415-435-5367
Linda Kramer, Executive Vice-President
Uma Ergil, Publicity Director

Stemmer House Publishers, Inc.
2627 Caves Road
Owings Mills, MD 21117
410-363-3690
Barbara Holdridge, President

Tambourine Books
See William Morrow & Co.

Thomson Learning
115 Fifth Avenue
New York, NY 10003
212-979-2210
Shirley C. Sarris, President
Frank Sloan, Editorial Director

Ticknor & Fields Books for Young Readers
215 Park Avenue South
New York, NY 10003
212-420-5800
Norma Jean Sawicki, Publisher
Kimberly Meyerson, Marketing Associate

Tiny Thought Press
1427 South Jackson Street
Louisville, KY 40217
800-456-3208
J. Martin Carraro, President
Bonita Dickey, Marketing Assistant

Verbal Images Press
19 Fox Hill Drive
Fairport, NY 14450

716-377-3807
Jeanne Gehret, President
Carolyn Loftin, Executive Assistant

Viking
See Penguin USA

Walker and Company
435 Hudson Street
New York, NY 10014
212-727-8300
Emily Easton, Editorial Director

Frederick Warne & Co., Inc.
See Penguin USA)

Franklin Watts Children's Book
See Grolier, Inc.

Western Publishing Co., Inc.
850 Third Avenue
New York, Ny 10022
212-753-8500
Pamela Davis, Publicity Manager

Albert Whitman & Co.
6340 Oakton Street
Morton Grove, IL 60053
708-581-0033
Kathleen Tucker, Children's Editor
Denise Ripp, School Library Marketing Director

John Wiley & Sons, Inc.
605 Third Avenue
New York, NY 10158
212-850-6000
Carole Hall, Editor-in-Chief

Workman Publishing Company
708 Broadway
New York, New York 10003
212-254-5900
Peter Workman, President
Suzanne Rafer, Editor-in-Chief

Zino Press Children's Books
2348 Pinehurst Drive
Middleton, WI 53562
608-836-6660
Joan Strasbaugh, Book Division Manager
Judith Laitman, Publisher

INDEX

Kathy East is Assistant Director and Head of Children's Services for the Wood County District Public Library in Bowling Green, Ohio. She has an M.L.S. from Wayne State University (Detroit, MI) and a B.A. from the University of Wisconsin-Madison. East has served as an adjunct faculty member of Kent State University conducting Library Science courses and workshops. She is active in the Ohio Library Council having served on the Board of Directors and then as president in 1987-88. She has also served on the Board and as president of the Association for Library Service to Children, a division of the American Library Association. Kathy East is also president of the Board of United Services for Effective Parenting (USEP-Ohio), a child advocacy group. She has served on numerous advisory boards involved in innovative services and professional growth for librarians. Kathy East is a regular presenter and workshop facilitator for conferences and meetings around the country.